PSYCHEDELICS

PETER STAFFORD

RONIN PUBLISHING
BERKELEY, CA
WWW.RONINPUB.COM

PSYCHEDELICS

TO SASHA

FOR FUTURE REFERENCE

Psychedelics

Published by
Ronin Publishing, Inc.
POBox 22900
Oakland, CA 94609
www.roninpub.com

Technical Editor:	Jeremy Bigwood
Reconfiguration Editor:	Beverly Potter
Copy & Layout Editor:	Amy Demmon
Molecular Diagrams:	Alexander Shulgin
Cover & Interior Design:	Beverly Potter
Cover Painting:	Clancy Cavnar

Library of Congress Card Number: 2003095498
Distributed to the book trade by **Publishers Group West**
Printed in the United States by **McNaughton & Gunn**

Material derived from Foreword, Introduction, Psychedelic Renaissance, Preview and Chapter One of *Psychedelics Encyclopedia*, third Expanded Edition

The author has made every effort to trace the ownership of all copyright and quoted material presented. In the event of any questions arising as to the use of a selection, Peter Stafford offers his apology for any errors or omissions that may inadvertently have occurred, and will make necessary corrections in future editions.

Acknowledgment and thanks are due the follow authors, agents, photographers, illustrators, and publishers for permission to use their materials.

Crawdaddy!, Harlan Reiders, R. Cobb, B. Madden, Frank Siteman, Lou Watts, Gloria Rovay, Claudio Naranjo, PharmChem, Carmen Helisten, Alexander Stafford, Ann & Sasha Shulgin, Arthur Brack, *Psychedelic Review, Journal of Psychedelic Drugs*, Berkeley Bonaparte, Parlay & Tina, Allen Ginsberg, Steve Gladstone, Humphry Osmond, Michael Horowitz, Dan Joy, John Beresford, Bonnie Golightly, *Journal of Psychoactive Drugs*, Albert Hofmann, Barry Crombe, Burns & MacEachern, Art Kleps, Jeremy Bigwood, Church of the Tree of Life, Peter Furst, Richard Evans Schultes, Robert Masters, Jean Houston, Robert Forte, Sigrid Radulovic, Chuck Silva, R.U. Sirius, Timothy Leary, R. Gordon Wasson, Sebastian Orfali, Oscar Janiger, Shasha Shulgin, Michael Shields, Beverly Potter, Bob Barker, Roland Greener, Rojelio Alcorcha, Bruce Eisner, Nona Sanford, Will Penna, Andy Weil, Jonathan Ott, John Lilly, Glen Perry, Rick Doblin, Carl Ruck, Stan Grof, Catherine Tompson Alan Watts, Myron Stolaroff, Stanley Krippner, Lester Grinspoon, James Bakalar, Stephen Gaskin, Aldous Huxley, Robert Anton Wilson, Ralph Metzner, Charlie Hass, Michael Hollingshed, Huston Smith, Walter Houston Clark, Frank Barron, Terence McKenna, PeterDemma & Ralph Abraham.

TABLE OF CONTENTS

psy·che·del·ic: *adj* [PSYCHE + Gr. *delein,* to make manifest] **1.** of or causing extreme changes in the conscious mind, as hallucinations, delusions, intensification of awarness and sensory perception, etc. **2.** of or associated with psychedelic drugs; specif., simulating the auditory or visual effects of the psychedelic state —n. a psychedelic drug.

INTRODUCTIONS

P ETER STAFFORD HAS DELVED INTO THE LITERATURE on psychedelic substances and produced an account of the properties attributed to them, how they are prepared and used, and the shifting social attitudes that have been displayed towards them. He has drawn as well on his personal experiences with the agents he discusses and the experiences of people he has known and talked to.

The result of this twin-pronged attack on the most perplexing intellectual problem and the most pervasive moral problem of the day—intellectual because of the difficulty in framing an adequate theory of the effect of psychedelic substances, moral because of their widespread use in contraven-tion of the law—is a book which stands in a class by itself.

It addresses the most perplexing intellectual problem and the most pervasive moral problem of the day.

This book does not solve any intellectual or moral problem, but it does something else. It goes a long way towards establishing what I think will be a dominant mode of looking at the effect of drugs like LSD. It does so by virtue of the equal importance it attaches to the oral and the literary sources of information and the equal stress it puts on observation and experience.

IMPORTANT ARCHIVES

THE LITERATURE ON THESE SUBSTANCES occupies a peculiar and seldom examined place in the record of humanity's search for knowledge. To begin with, it is not clear exactly what it is about. Humphry Osmond coined *psychedelic* as a better way of saying what *hallucinogenic* and *psychotomimetic* had been used to say before.

Unfortunately, the term *mind-manifesting* is at least as confusing as *hallucination* and *psychosis* are, to say nothing of a state which supposedly mimics psychosis. Calling something *psychedelic* merely suggests a similarity perceived by people who experience the effect of first one psychedelic drug and then another. That is a rather loose unifying principle. Then there is the literature's unusual scope. It embraces parts of neurochemistry, psychology, religion, clinical medicine, botany, and a variety of other topics which it has trouble housing under one roof.

CONTRADICTIONS

THE LANGUAGE IT IS WRITTEN IN CAN BE INSPIRING or debased. Just who an expert is is hard to tell. Some of the most aberrant thinking has been expressed in academic journals of the highest quality, and some of the sanest and most lucid in the underground street rags. In fact, the scientific credentials of an author tend to ensure that a large proportion of what he or she writes will consist of nonsense.

The literature is notorious for the contradictions it contains. Hardly anything has been stated in it which has not been somewhere flatly contradicted. So it is no wonder that the literature and with it the psychedelic substances themselves have gained an unsavory reputation in academic circles and that by and large academic research with them has got nowhere, while startling findings are described by off-beat and fringe investigators.

PARTICIPATORY INVESTIGATIONS

THIS BRINGS UP A SECOND DIFFICULTY. The best research and the best writing in the field have been done by people who have more than once exposed themselves to the effect of the agents they are dealing with. This introduces a novel principle into pharmacology, i.e. that understanding the effect of the psychedelic class of drugs is conditional on personal experience with them. Naturally, it has been vigorously contested. A doctor does not need to experience the effect of insulin to understand and treat diabetes. A judge does not need to have been a plaintiff or a defendant to hand down a good judgement. But a special case can be made for psychedelics

The argument goes approximately as follows: One way of explaining the effect of LSD is that the person who experiences it gains access to a range of information not normally available to him. The inrush of new knowledge so enhances his state of consciousness that his perception of people and objects in the world is no longer the same. The further outcome is a shift in his world-view, so that even after the normal conscious state has been restored the frame of reference he used to regard things in no longer seems comfortable or right. A new frame of reference has been acquired which does feel right, because it includes the old view-point within the new, more comprehensive one.

> *Understanding the effect of the psychedelic class of drugs is conditional on personal experience with them.*

DISPUTE

ALONG THIS LINE OF REASONING, a dispute between two investigators, one who has and one who has not personally encountered the effect of such a drug, soon makes the latter feel irritated and leads him to dismiss the statements of the "experienced" investigator as examples of woolly thinking. He may even go further and dub the

Stafford's credibility is enhanced by his wide experience.

other as a victim of brain-washing, someone whose power of thinking critically has been injured by drug-use— this is the *toxic psychosis* thesis.

At the same time, the LSD-experienced investigator can point to limitations in the observations of the inexperienced and in the conclusions he inevitably draws from them. I leave it to the reader to decide how sensible this argument is. My own view is that while the idea that you have to take a psychedelic drug to come to grips with its effect may sound far-fetched, there are solid grounds for conceding it, so that the credibility of a writer like Peter Stafford is enhanced by his wide experience with psychedelics, and definitely not lessened.

HISTORICAL THREAD

WHAT ELSE ADDS TO THIS BOOK'S SOUNDNESS? One attraction for me is the historical thread running through it. More than other writers, Peter saw the importance of recording the events that took place in the early days. No one else would do the job, so Peter took it on himself, as early as 1960, preserving anything in print, documenting events, taping interviews, and corresponding with anyone who would write back. The Stafford Collection is deposited in the library of Columbia University, by the way.

Well before 1960 centers of LSD-activity were springing up everywhere. Oscar Janiger gave sessions in little cubicles in his office in Los Angeles. In Menlo Park Myron Stolaroff and his colleagues gave sessions under the grandiloquently yet after all aptly-named International Institute for Advanced Studies. By 1963, 500 sessions using high-dose LSD had been completed and people were arriving at the doors of the center from all over the continent. Regina Duncan Blewett and Nick Chwelos elucidated the course of the normal LSD session in their unjustly neglected and now-lost masterpiece *A Handbook for the Use of LSD in Psychotherapy.*

Such cases of research—a list is bound to be invidi-
ous—began to come to the attention of people tuned in
to their significance and Peter sooner or later got to hear
about them. A number of Peter's historical references are
original in the sense that they are recollections of events
he participated in or people or places he encountered.

A FRIENDSHIP

I MET PETER IN NEW YORK NEAR THE END OF 1966, when
he was writing his first book on LSD with Bonnie
Golightly. At that time Chuck Bick was the city's chief
supplier. Chuck's customers included bankers, lawyers,
doctors, teaching staff from New York and Columbia
Universities, writers, musicians, painters, playboys, clergy-
men, call girls—as he related it the list seemed endless,
though the number of purchasers was small.

His method of obtaining LSD was simple. When
stock ran low, Chuck phoned Sandoz in New Jersey and
told the doctor there who handled LSD that this was Dr.
Bick with a request for an additional vial of 10 milli-
grams, and could his assistant stop by in the afternoon to
pick it up? Sheila, Chuck's wife, drove over to the plant
and collected it. Chuck had no problem getting LSD,
and, as far as I could tell, his people had no trouble
taking it.

When I met Peter, he did not know these people,
but we discovered that we knew people who knew each
other, and a circle of friendships was formed with links
continuing down to the present day. Considering how
disturbing the whole question of LSD was to become, I
find it instructive to recall how tranquil it was then. The
expected attitude was casual and vaguely positive. LSD was
looked on as a benign substance with a number of not-
so-well-explored potential applications. The polemics which
succeeded the Harvard furor in 1963 and 1964 were
definitely absent.

LEARY'S IMPACT

1963 WAS THE TURNING POINT. By mid-1963, Timothy Leary had emerged from obscurity and was about to turn the philanthropic idealism of the time into a unfortunate debacle. Tim had a lot of good ideas—he was incapable of turning off the stream—which he was impatient to see work. There were prisoner projects, divinity student projects, projects for radicalizing the Psychology Department, for starting a journal, for flooding the world with propaganda extolling the power of the love pill.

Tim's fierce determination was his belief in his ability to create a political force which would overhaul the composition of the government of the United States. He would have accomplished this aim when enough people had experienced the effect of LSD and undergone the change of conscious state which would permanently affect their outlook for the better—prejudice giving way to brotherly concern, destructive ego trips to coexistence.

Tim's urgent priority was therefore to arrange for as many people to take LSD as possible. His sensibility was basically religious, though the direction he moved in was political. Tim was out to change the State, his strategy being confrontation and his weapon a chemical substance which he called a sacrament. He vowed that in ten years a million Americans would win "internal freedom"—the Fifth Freedom, freedom to control one's central nervous system.

UNAVOIDABLE REACTION

BUT THE CHEMICAL INSURRECTION HE SO BOLDLY PLANNED produced an unavoidable reaction. Each escalation organized by Tim and the thousands, even millions, who eventually sympathized with him was faced with an equal and opposite response by the conservative forces in the country who watched what he was doing with mounting alarm. The more Tim praised LSD, the more they trounced it. Tim said it saved souls. They said it promoted suicide and murder.

A succession of LSD-inspired confrontations and counter-confrontations is discernable in the history of the '60s and early '70s. Jack Kennedy was on the Board of Regents of Harvard University when Dick Alpert got kicked out and Tim followed. If the game plan had been different, Jack might have been the first American President to take LSD, for his brother Robert is believed to have been taking either LSD or psilocybin in the spring of 1963 and entertaining foreign dignitaries with it in his apartment in New York and probably thus to have been saying good things about the drug to Jack.

But with the confrontation tactics coming out of Harvard, Jack had good reason to hesitate. And five years later, with well over a million Americans thoroughly frightened and put off, President Johnson was singling LSD out for denunciation in his State of the Union message to Congress. Johnson's vow was to rid the nation of the menace he saw LSD to be. Conceivably, Johnson's intransigence in his policy over Vietnam was motivated by his fear or hatred of the voice of people who were vaunting LSD and psychedelic drugs in general.

Leary's sensibility was religious; the direction he moved was political.

YIPPIE MANIFESTO

AT ANY RATE, at a party in the East Village three weeks before Johnson addressed Congress a new escalation of the process of confrontation was shaping up. The celebration was for the New Year, 1968. The guests, who later were to claim a good deal of attention as the "Chicago Seven," were examining the possibility of doing something to stop the violence in Vietnam. The punch they drank contained not alcohol but LSD. The thoughts they entertained in consequence were far-reaching and ultrapractical. The manifesto coming out of that evening's work was the "Yippie Manifesto," and it set in motion the long train of events which exploded in the violence in Chicago, when Johnson lost the nomination and his Presidency.

NIXON AND LSD

BUT THAT WAS NOT THE END. Under Nixon, Johnson's campaign to stamp out LSD was carried on to extreme lengths. There was talk of introducing the death penalty for persons convicted of possession. The climax of the U.S. government's war on LSD was staged in Vienna with the signing of the International Convention abolishing its use. At home, a case can be made for the idea that Nixon's excesses were committed primarily against those with links to the pro-drug, anti-war movement—for these were two faces of the same desire. At length, some sort of naturally occurring homeostasis seems to have restored a balance. Nixon and LSD both disappeared, each one having cancelled out the other.

I wanted to go into this not to make a point that Tim's obstinacy led to Nixon's downfall, which is true, nor to raise the question whether the use of LSD as a political instrument was justifiable, which is debatable, but to suggest that the price paid for the insurrection Tim devised was the interruption of supplies of LSD and in due course the flooding of the market with a variety of toxic substitutes labelled "acid." This brings me back to Peter Stafford and my belief that the point of view he represents is the right one for now.

CONFRONTATION IS ALIEN

THE TIME FOR CONFRONTATION IS PAST, if it was ever present. Peter is made of softer, more ductile stuff than Tim. He poses no threat to anyone and is not about to get under anybody's skin. Tim had his day and history will honor him for the heroic man he was. Peter epitomizes the unheroic plodder with no particular qualifications, and we feel more comfortable with him. In fact, there is something alien in confrontation to the whole ethos of LSD and its sister-substances. Non-confrontation is a cardinal feature of a well-run LSD session.

Johnson vowed to rid the nation of the menace he saw LSD to be.

Confrontation is precisely what should be avoided when a person who has taken LSD shows signs of agitation or depression or in some other way is manifesting resistance to the natural flow of the experience. What the person helping him can do then is search for

Tim's obstinacy led to Nixon's downfall.

or suggest an image or idea which complements the image or idea which acted as the springboard of resistance. Negative emotions are thereby not provoked but rather calmed. The resistance is undone and the normal flow of the session can proceed.

MYTHIC

LAST, THERE IS A MYTHIC ELEMENT in the emergence of LSD and other psychedelic drugs which Peter's book exemplifies. Eileen Garrett told me a story which I have not found recorded in her writing and which I do not now recall the details of precisely. The gist of it is that she fell down in the bathroom of her apartment and imagined she was dying. In a trance she had a vision in which old Dr. Sandoz, patriarch of the firm in Basel, appeared and told her that a chemical substance with a power to bring great benefit to the world had been discovered in his laboratory. When Mrs. Garrett recovered from her trance, she recalled that Dr. Sandoz had been dead for seven years. (I do not know the date of his death, but it could serve to pinpoint the date of his appearance in the vision.)

As I remember her words, Mrs. Garrett did not then know what LSD was and it was only later, when she heard reports of LSD and the part played in its synthesis by Dr. Hofmann, that she understood the words heard in her trance. Be that as it may, the good, in some people's eyes, that LSD and members of the psychedelic family of drugs can help bring about is the revelation of the hidden depths of human consciousness. An instrument is now at hand which tells us things about ourselves which we may misguidedly think we do not want to know and would prefer to leave in the depth where for all but a few individuals they have always been, but which in reality offer us the greatest help in broadening our understanding of and deepening our feeling for ourselves and the world around us.

HUMAN CONSCIOUSNESS

PETER IS ON THE SIDE OF THOSE WHO ARE COMMITTED to what is now a world-wide trend, exploration of the structure and the

━━━━━━━━ function of human consciousness, a search of
The thaw will which the use of psychedelics is an integral
    come.   part. He wants LSD back in the laboratory, the clinic, the place of meditation, on the street, wherever it belongs. Social controls will be needed for distribution of psychedelics. The details can be worked out. But we are not going to keep LSD and the rest of the consciousness-revealing drugs on ice indefinitely. The thaw will come.

—John Beresford, M.D.

THE SHULGINS' PERSPECTIVE

PSYCHEDELICS IS A COLLECTION OF PHOTOGRAPHS, history, sources and the descriptions of the many plants and preparations of the treasures that we have in our psychedelic information inventory.

The remarkable mental effects of LSD and the many pharmacologically related psychedelic drugs have been studied, celebrated, or condemned by many groups with emphasis not on the source of the activity, but on the activity itself.

MANY VIEWS

THIS IS VIEWED AND EVALUATED THROUGH MANY DIFFERENT EYES. The historian's start might well be the Greek world of Eleusis, or the influence of Soma on the Asian cultural development. The sociologists are the archivists of the group behavior at Millbrook and the Haight Ashbury scene during the Summer of Love in San Francisco. Various governmental agencies tried to make use of this remarkable psychedelic activity for a broad spectrum of needs. The CIA and the U.S. military have looked at it as a truth serum, as a potential chemical warfare weapon, and Congress looks upon it as a threat to public health and writes laws prohibiting its sources.

Botanists use it as an exploration guide to natural sources, from cacti to Morning Glory seeds. Yjese substances are seen as a source of sacrament or of mysticism by many people in several religious faiths such as the Native American Church or the Brazilian Church, the U.D.V. (Unias de Vegetalis). Chemists and biochemists strive to correlate this activity with chemical structure and neurotransmitter interactions, with the hope of the development of some agent that might have medical utility. And the medical community initially explored agents with this psychotropic activity in the treatment of alcoholism, as a psychotherapeutic tool.

Stafford has blended many views in this Work.

The value of this book is in its presentation of how these many points of view blended with one another, or came into conflict, as the public attitude evolved from curiosity to fascination, to something close to hysteria. With *Psychedelics*, Peter Stafford reveals a complex and multifaceted aspect of the American political, social and medical scene as it reacted to the appearance of this unanticipated challenge called psychedelic drugs.

—Sasha & Ann Shulgin

WEIL'S PERSPECTIVE

PSYCHEDELIC DRUGS AND THE PLANTS THEY COME FROM constitute a distinct pharmacological group, all of which stimulate the central and sympathetic nervous systems and all of which affect serotonin or dopamine pathways (or both) in the brain. These drugs are also distinguished by great medical safety. They do not kill, injure or produce any serious physical toxicity even in large overdoses or chronic use over lifetimes. Despite much desire and activity on the part of some scientists, reporters and governmental agencies to come up with damning evidence of harm, the true psychedelics still look like the safest drugs known to medicine.

I refer to medical safety only. There are dangers of psychedelic plants and chemicals having to do with acute psychological toxicity—that is, bad trips. These reactions are more the product of set and setting than of pharmacology. Their probability of occurrence can be reduced to a minimum by careful attention to the

Like me, Stafford finds psychedelics totally fascinating from many different perspectives.

purity of the substances, dosage, time and place of use, and availability of experienced guides. Employed intelligently, they are not only safe but also sometimes highly beneficial, since they have the potential to produce dramatic cures of both mental and physical problems as well as to provide experiences of great personal value to some persons. Finally, the abuse potential of the true psychedelics is quite low. They are almost never associated with dependence, and very few people use them in destructive ways. Stafford explains them fully and gives a good description of their positive potential.

Like me, Stafford finds psychedelics totally fascinating from many different perspectives, including those of botany, chemistry, psychology, anthropology, sociology, religion, politics, and the law. Most than most substances in our world, psychedelics touch on many vital areas of human life and so can teach us much about ourselves, whether we use them or not, promote them or crusade against them, study them or just like to read about them.

—Andrew Weil, M.D.

I

PSYCHEDELIC ROOTS

H UMPHRY OSMOND PROPOSED THE TERM *psychedelic* while in correspondence with the novelist Aldous Huxley. The word comes from the Greek word *psyche,* which means soul, and *delein,* which means to make manifest, or *deloun,* which means to show or reveal.

Huxley invented the word *phanerothyme* and encased it in a couplet for Osmond's consideration. Huxley proclaimed, "To make this trivial world sublime. Take half a gramme of phanerothyme." Osmond thought that the word Huxley selected was *too* beautiful and replied with, "To fathom hell or soar angelic. Just take a pinch of psychedelic."

Especially noteworthy about the word *psychedelic* is the presence of the first *e*—which varies from the ordinary way of combining Greek roots, and, thus, dissociates this word from the misleading connotations of psychotic. "Soul-manifesting" belongs to the category of meanings that make sense in

Psychedelic means soul-manifesting

terms of contrast. Just as empty implies full, as child implies adult, so soul-manifesting implies an enlargement or actualization of consciousness.

INTOXICATION

THE WORD *INTOXICATION* HAS MORE SYNONYMS than any other word in English, but none conveys the essence of a psychedelic mental state. To be "psychedelicized" is not at all the same as being drunk.

Intoxication by alcohol may hint at the experience that is characteristic of psychedelics. Hermann Hesse speaks of alcohol in *Steppenwolf* as being capable of "lighting the golden trail." William James wrote about the impulse intoxication gives to mystical feeling and "Yeasaying." However, intoxication does not approach the revelatory power of psychedelics. Its well-known drawbacks—loss of lucidity and sometimes of memory—must put it into a different category from LSD. If any of the *intoxication* synonyms are to be used to describe soul-manifested states, the best is probably *inebriation*, because it lacks the connotation of poisoning contained in the root *toxi-*.

Pychedelic Drug

A psychedelic drug is one which, without causing physical addiction, craving, major physiological disturbances, delirium, disorientation, or amnesia, more or less reliably produces thought, mood, and perceptual changes otherwise rarely experienced except in dreams, contemplative and religious exaltation, flashes of vivid involuntary memory, and acute psychoses.

—Lester Grinspoon & James B. Bakalar
Psychedelic Drugs Reconsidered

HALLUCINOGEN

HALLUCINOGEN IS COMMONLY USED TO DESCRIBE substances producing a psychedelic experience. There is some truth in the characterization, for trippers often see "visions," especially with the eyes closed. However, the hallucinatory effect is only one part of the experience—often a minor part.

Humphry Osmond

Richard Evans Schultes and Albert Hofmann weighed

the various descriptive terms and settled on the use of *hallucinogenic* and *hallucinogen* in their books, while pointing out how inaccurate they are. Similarly, chemist Alexander Shulgin, after explaining that most MDA-like compounds evoke no visual imagery at all, labeled them hallucinogenic substances in his writings.

NARCOTIC

Ethnobotanist William Emboden retained the title *Narcotic Plants* in the second edition of his book on the botany of psychedelics, even though these psychedelic plants and related compounds are quite the opposite of narcotics. Unlike opiates, they are stimulating, and they are non-addictive. Psychedelics also differ from ordinary stimulants; they increase lucidity, generally, but not, as with amphetamine, at the expense of psychological warmth.

PSYCHOTOMIMETIC

The most common early psychiatric term for the soul-manifesting botanicals and compounds has been *psychotomimetic*, stemming from a concept proposed in the late 19th Century by the French doctor J. J. Moreau de Tours. He was the first to raise the hope that chemicals could produce insights toward the alleviation of mental illness. That hope was only partially realized.

While the psychedelic state may have some similarities to psychotic ones, the differences are more numerous and more significant. A main difference is that the induced state is known to last only a short while. By the 1960s, few of the therapeutic projects using psychedelics were attempting to bring about psychotic mental states. Yet the term still lingers, with papers describing blissful, beneficial results ascribed to a "psychosis-mimicking" drug.

PSYCHOLYTIC

ANOTHER PSYCHOTHERAPEUTIC TERM with much currency, especially in Europe, is *psycholytic*. It was specifically limited to refer only to low-dosage use of psychedelics in conjunction with therapeutic sessions. Shulgin has compiled several more descriptors from the prominent psychotherapeutic literature—*delirients, delusionogens, dysleptics, misperceptionogens, mysticomimetics, phantasticants, pharmakons, psychotaraxics, psychoticants, psychotogens* and *schizogens*. Researchers have often favored Louis Lewin's suggestion of *phantastica,* but it has never really caught on.

ENTHEOGEN

SEVERAL WRITERS TURNED TO GERMAN OR SANSKRIT to find a more appropriate descriptive word. More notable terms are *peak experiences,* a term popularized by the psychologist Abraham Maslow; *altered states,* used by the psychologist Charles Tart; *alternative states,* coined by Norman Zinberg; and *cosmic experience,* featured in William James' *The Varieties of Religious Experience.*

The term *entheogen* was proposed by the team of Ruck, Bigwood, Staples, Ott, and Wasson, writing in a 1979 issue of *The Journal of Psychedelic Drugs.* They argued that not only is *psychedelic* an incorrect verbal formulation, mixing Greek and Latin roots, but it has become so invested with connotations of the pop-culture of the 1960s that it is incongruous to speak of a shaman's taking a psychedelic drug. The term *entheogen,* they argued, is appropriate for describing states of shamanic and ecstatic possession induced by ingestion of mind-altering drugs.

In Greek the word *entheos* means "god within," and was used to describe when one is inspired and possessed by the god that has entered one's body. It was applied to prophetic seizures, erotic passion, and artistic creation, as well as to those religious rites in which mystical states were experienced through the ingestion of substances that were transsubstantial with the deity. Combining this Greek root with *gen,* "which denotes the action of 'becoming,'" they argued further for the suitability of *entheogen.*

Entheogen

Our word sits easily on the tongue and seems quite natural in English.... We could speak of entheogens *or, in an adjectival form, of* **entheogenic** *plants or substances. In a strict sense, only those vision-producing drugs that can be shown to have figured in shamanic or religious rites would be designated entheogens, but in a looser sense, the term could also be applied to other drugs, both natural and artificial, that induce alterations of consciousness similar to those documented for ritual ingestion of traditional entheogens.*

In Greek, entheos means "god within."

Entheogen has evolved into the preferred term used in the ethnobotanical literature. So far as popular usage is concerned, it doesn't seem to sit as easily on the tongue as originally claimed.

VARIETIES OF PSYCHEDELICS

THE TERM PSYCHEDELIC IS STILL USED for many plants and synthetic compounds that produce similar changes in the ordinary functioning of consciousness. Exactly which substances should be included in this category, and which should not, has been a subject of considerable controversy for several reasons. The main difficulty is that there are several components to the psychedelic experience, appearing in different combinations and intensities with each drug.

If one tries to index psychoactivity according to response to color, for example, then the MDA and marijuana compound-clusters would be excluded by some. Many people would also exclude marijuana because it has a different chemistry from most of the others and acts more subtly. However, for some people its use can be inspiring, and it has widened the scope of the mind for many.

Aside from the variations among mind-altering compounds, there are variations among users to consider.
Some people seem especially sensitive to a very wide
range of substances. Jean Cocteau felt quickening, mind-
and soul-manifesting effects from opiates. The creative response he showed to those drugs, however, is rare.

Glenn T. Perry

Perhaps the easiest way to distinguish a compound as psyche-delic is by means of two primary mental criteria. It induces enlargements in the scope of the mind, and these enlarge-ments or new perceptions are influenced and focused by
one's mind set and by the session setting. Osmond has
provided a broad but usable definition of enlargements,
saying that "the brain ... acts more subtly and complexly
than when it is normal."

Mind set, usually shortened to *set*, refers to attitudes,
preparations, preoccupations, and feelings toward the drug
and toward other people in attendance at a psychedelic
session. *Setting* refers to the complex set of things in a
session's immediate surroundings, which include time of
day, weather, sounds or music, and other environmental
factors. If results don't vary considerably with differing
sets and settings, a compound almost certainly isn't a
psychedelic.

2

ERGOT DISCOVERED

I N 1960, ALBERT HOFMANN ANALYZED the constituents of certain Morning Glory seeds and declared that *Rivea (Turbina) corymbosa* contained ergot alkaloids. This information was hard for the scientific world to accept because: previous chemical analysis, recommended in 1955 by Osmond after self-experimentation with Morning Glory seeds, had shown no psychoactive principles, and, secondly, until that time ergot alkaloids had been found only in the rye fungus *Claviceps purpurea*, which belongs in an entirely unrelated wing of the plant kingdom.

"Chemotaxonomically," said Schultes, commenting on the unexpected discovery of lysergic acid amides in Morning Glories, "such an occurrence would be highly unlikely." Hence, many research-ers suspected that spores from fungi already in Hofmann's lab had somehow invaded the tissues of the Morning Glories examined. Later, however, chemical analyses substantiated Hofmann's claim.

Rye—host for ergot fungus.

PRINCIPAL AGENT

THE PRINCIPLE AGENT in the Morning Glory plant was found to be a *d*-lysergic acid amide, which had already been synthesized, and was known as both ergine and LA-111. Other alkaloids of lesser importance found to be psychoactively influential in *Turbina corymbosa* were *d*-isolysergic acid amide, or isoergine, chanoclavine, elymoclavine, and lysergol.

The lysergic acid used for the synthesis of LSD was originally obtained from a rye-attacking fungus called *Claviceps purpurea.* The sclerotium, or fruiting body, of this filamentous fungus is known as ergot and contains the "skeleton" for making the psychoactive molecule. Many times during the Middle Ages, and on other occasions up until the first quarter of the last century, it was baked, inadvertently, into bread. Those who ate it felt the terrifying, sometimes deadly, consequences of ergot poisoning, which appeared in gangrenous and convulsive forms and was often called "St. Anthony's fire." People thus affected often experienced ecstasies, but frequently they went into a "St. Vitus dance." Sometimes bodily extremities blackened and fell off. Thousands died.

Raven, Evert, and Curtis in their *Biology of Plants* note that in one such epidemic in 994 AD, more than 40,000 died. In 1722, ergotism struck down the cavatry of Czar Peter the Great on the eve of battle for the conquest of Turkey, and thus changed the course of history.

When it was realized in the 17th Century that ergot-infected rye baked into bread was the cause of these outbreaks, they became less frequent and less extensive. The last ergot epidemic occurred in southern Russia during 1926-1927.

A popular book and many writers have erroneously described a mass poisoning in 1951 in the southern French city of Pont-St. Esprit as the result

Arthur Bracke

Ergot growing on rye

of ergotism. Thirty people felt that they were being pursued by demons and snakes, and five died. The cause, however, was actually an organic mercury compound that had been used to disinfect seeds.

Germinating sclerotium of ergot of rye

M. Wilson: *Ergot & Ergotism*

Sclerotia

At least thirty alkaloids appear in different kinds of ergot, varying in strength and chemical arrangements with the host medium, the weather, and other local circumstances. The most common are "peptide alkaloids" of an ergotamine-ergotoxine grouping—not soluble in water—and these have been responsible for the two forms of ergotism. The other alkaloids are lysergic acid amides—which are water soluble—the most important being ergine, or *d*-lysergic acid amide, and ergonovine, or *d*-lysergic acid-1-2-propanolamide. The latter was isolated independently by four groups of researchers in the 1930s and thus was variously known as ergometrine, ergobasin, ergotocine, or ergostetrine.

Fully-developed capitula

DID THE ANCIENT GREEKS TRIP?

THESE DISTINCTIONS OF BOTANICAL CHEMISTRY are important to this story because of a challenging question R. Gordon Wasson posed to Hofmann in July 1975: Could early man in ancient Greece have hit on a method to isolate an hallucinogen from ergot that would have given him an experience comparable to LSD or psilocybin?

Hofmann's response a year later was yes, such effects could have occurred with ergot grown on wheat or barley—rye wasn't known in ancient Greece—and noted that an even easier way would have been to use the ergot growing on the common wild grass *Paspalum*. On April 1, 1976, Hofmann confirmed such a possibility when he took an oral dose of 2 mg. of ergonovine maleate, equivalent to about 1.5 mg. of the ergonovine base, which is about six times the normal dose used in medicine for postpartum hemorrhaging. He found that this dose produced mild psychedelic activity that lasted more than five hours.

SECRET OF THE MYSTERIES

EVIDENCE MARSHALLED for an entheogenic interpretation of the "Elunsnian Mysteries" by Wasson, Hofmann, and the Greek scholar Carl A.P. Ruck, along with a new translation of the *Homeric Hymn to Demeter,* appears in their *The Road to Eleusis: Unveiling the Secret of the Mysteries.* They demonstrate that the potion used for more than 2,000 years in these annual "mysteries"—mysterious to the uninitiated because the penalty for revealing the ceremony was death—involved water infusions of infected

> The Mysteries were an experience, rather than something learned.

barley and the sclerotium of *Claviceps paspali* growing on the wild grass *Paspalum distichum,* which flourished throughout the area and particularly on the nearby Rarian plain. The complex historical reconstruction of these events, in the words of Jonathan Ott, "for the first time places the sacred mushroom [of ergot] in our own cultural past."

Hofmann wrote in his autobiography, "The cultural-historical meaning of the Eleusinian Mysteries, their influence on European intellectual history, can scarcely be overestimated. Here suffering humankind found a cure for its rational, objective, cleft intellect, in a mystical totality experience, that let it believe in immortality, in an everlasting existence."

TRANFORMATIVE RITES

UP TO 3,000 PEOPLE ANNUALLY were initiated "in a perfect way" for two millenia, until the suppression of these rites under Christianity in the 4th Century AD. Anyone who could speak Greek and who hadn't committed murder could present themselves once for this initiation.

Half a year of preparatory rituals began in the spring, culminating in September in a procession lasting several days from Athens to the temple at Eleusis. The ceremony occurred at night; ancient writers hint that important things were *seen*—in a room "totally unsuited for theatrical performances," as Ruck described the temple. Among those initiated were Aristotle, Sophocles, Plato, Aeschylus, Cicero, Pindar, and possibly even Homer, plus many Roman emperors such as Hadrian and Marcus Arelius.

Aristides the Rhetor in the 2nd Century AD called the experience "new, astonishing, inaccessible to rational cognition." The *Homeric Hymn to Demeter,* which tells us most about what occurred, states: "Blissful is he among men on Earth who has beheld that! He who has not been initiated into the holy Mysteries, who has had no part therein, remains a corpse in gloomy darkness." Pindar remarked, "Blissful is he who after having beheld this enters on the way beneath the Earth. He knows the end of life as well as its divinely granted beginning." Cicero said of Eleusis: "Not only have we received the reason there that we may live in joy, but also, besides, that we may die with better hope." Aristotle revealed only that these Mysteries were *an experience,* rather than something learned.

As far as I know, nobody since *The Road to Eleusis* appeared in 1978 has an aqueous solution of ergot been used—which is understandable, given the history of ergotism. On the other hand, *Paspalum distichum,* as described by Hofmann, contains only alkaloids that are hallucinogenic and which could even have been used directly in powder form.

A REPLICATION

IN 1979, JEREMY BIGWOOD, Jonathan Ott, Catherine Thompson, and Patricia Neely reported in the *Journal of Psychedelic Drugs* on their attempt to replicate Hofmann's finding in three experiments with ergonovine maleate, each time in a pastoral setting. They were following up Wasson and Ruck, who tried the same amount as Hofmann, but they did not experience distinct entheogenic effects.

With Thompson acting as a guide, three of them took 3 mg. of ergonovine maleate, which appeared as a slightly phosphorescent bluish solution in water. Fifteen minutes later they felt like lying down and looking at the sky. Then there were "very mild visual alterations, characterized by perception of an 'alive' quality in inanimate objects." Most of this effect passed within an hour. When walking along the beach, they experienced mild leg cramps. Bigwood saw eidetic imagery before going to bed, and the three "slept easily...awakening refreshed in the morning."

Claviceps purpurea

 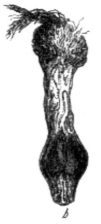 

| A very young ovary of rye in the Sphacelia stage. (x8) | Older ovary, with the Sphacelia in its upper part, while the sclerotium is being formed in the lower. (x5) | Longitudinal section through the same stage as b. (x5) |

Ergot & Ergotism

The three experimenters were convinced that ergonovine was psychoactive, but only Bigwood was persuaded the drug was entheogenic. They decided to try it again two weeks later in an increased dosage of 5 mg., though Neely took only 3.75 mg. "Again, we experienced lassitude and leg cramps, more pronounced than in the earlier experiment." The psychic effects were more intense than previously, particularly eidetic imagery. "Now it was clear to all of us that ergonovine was entheogenic....The entheogenic effects, however, were very mild, while the somatic effects were quite strong. We had none of the euphoria characteristic of LSD and psilocybin experiences."

To determine if higher consciousness alteration was possible, they tried larger oral doses of ergonovine maleate a week later. This time, Neely took a dose of 7.5 mg. and the others took 10 mg.

Psychic Effects

J.O. described "lashes in periphery, ringing in ears, inner restlessness" 40 minutes after ingestion, and later noted "mild hallucinosis, cramps in legs" [and] felt the cramping in the legs as painful and debilitating. The psychic effects did not increase with the same magnitude as the somatic effects.... For what seemed like hours, we lay on our backs atop a small pumphouse, watching fluffy cumulus clouds pass silently above us. The effects were still quite intense six hours after ingestion. One of us experienced abundant eidetic imagery, rapidly-changing, colorful geometric patterns, undulating, never still. We all had a slight hangover the following morning.

—Bigwood, Ott, Thompson

3

HOFMANN DISCOVERS LSD

OF ALL SUBSTANCES THAT EXCITE the visionary powers of the mind, LSD is the most potent. It belongs to a class of substances that can be divided into two groups. One group occurs naturally, in the fungus ergot and in members of the Woodrose and Morning Glory families. The other group is produced semi-synthetically, the most important member being LSD. Both groups exhibit a four-ring crystalline chemical structure. LSD-type compounds are all amides.

In a curious circle of coincidence, knowledge about the psychoactivity of the natural group came along only after the synthesis of LSD by Hofmann. Unlike most chemists, who work mainly with synthetics, at the end of the 1920s Hofmann was drawn toward study of natural substances. Under the supervision of Dr. Arthur Stoll, who isolated the first ergot alkaloid in a pure chemical form, Hofmann synthesized a number of ergot analogs, or closely related compounds, at Sandoz Pharmaceuticals in Basel, Switzerland.

Hofmann was the first human to experience LSD.

FIRST LSD EXPERIENCES

HOFMANN'S LABORATORY SYNTHESES of ergot analogs resulted in the construction of many new lysergic acid derivatives. Several turned out to be useful in medicine—especially in obstetrics, geriatrics, and the treatment of migraine headaches. The twenty-fifth compound in the series his team produced—lab coded

LSD-25—was expected on the basis of its molecular structure to be a circulatory and respiratory stimulant. Tested on experimental animals in 1938, it made them restless and caused them to display "strong uterine-constricting effects." Because these results were not of sufficient interest to the Sandoz staff, further testing ceased.

In the spring of 1943, Hofmann received "a peculiar presentiment." He felt that LSD-25 might possess properties other than those observed in Sandoz's initial investigation and set about resynthesizing this substance, intending to resubmit it to Sandoz's pharmacological department for further examination. That was "in a way uncommon," he wrote in his autobiography, "for experimental substances

An ampule of Sandoz LSD.

were as a rule definitely stricken from the research program, if they were once found uninteresting from the pharmacological aspect."

FIRST HUMAN EXPERIENCE

IN THE COURSE OF RECRYSTALLIZING only a few centigrams, or hundredths of a gram, for analysis, a strange thing happened to Hofmann.

> I suddenly became strangely inebriated. The external world became changed as in a dream. Objects appeared to gain in relief; they assumed unusual dimensions; and colors became more glowing. Even self-perception and the sense of time were changed. When the eyes were closed, there surged upon me an uninterrupted stream of fantastic images of extraordinary plasticity and vividness and accompanied by an intense, kaleidoscope-like play of colors. After about two hours, the not unpleasant inebriation, which had been experienced whilst I was fully conscious, disappeared.

ONE DROP

HOFMANN WAS THE FIRST HUMAN TO EXPERIENCE LSD, an
accident that should never have occurred under careful
laboratory conditions. "It was possible that a drop had
fallen on my fingers and had been absorbed by the skin,"
he noted. One drop.

The most powerful psychedelic agent known at that
time was mescaline. To receive a psychedelic effect, the
average human body has to absorb a third of a gram or
more of mescaline. However, LSD is about four thousand
times stronger than mescaline. A drop on his skin was
enough—perhaps 20-50 micrograms, millionths of a gram,
abbreviated "mcg."—to give Hofmann a light trip lasting
noticeably for only two hours. If LSD were only a thousand times as strong as mescaline, Hofmann would
probably not have felt its mental effects. But he did
notice. Three days later he resolved to apply methodical
analysis to his accidental discovery.

A cautious man, Hofmann started by ingesting a
quarter of a milligram, 250 mcg., intending to increase
the dosage as necessary to complete a full description of
the effects of the drug. That at least was his intention.

Jeremy Bigwood

Albert Hofmann

Forty minutes after
administration of the
conservative first dose,
less than fifty words
along in his efforts to
record observations, came
a far more powerful
reaction—the first inten-
tional human experience
of LSD. Hofmann was
unable to continue his
description in the lab
notebook as "the last
words could only be
written with great
difficulty....I asked my

laboratory assistant to accompany me home as I believed that my condition would be a repetition of the disturbance of the previous Friday. While we were still cycling home, however, it became clear that the symptoms were much stronger than the first time. I had great difficulty in speaking coherently, my field of vision swayed before me, and objects appeared distorted like the images in curved mirrors. I had the impression of being unable to move from the spot, although my assistant told me afterwards that we had cycled at a good pace...."

> *April 19, 1943: Preparation of an 0.05% aqueous solution of d-lysergic acid diethylamide tartrate.*
> *4:20 PM: 0.05 cc. (0.25 mg. LSD) [250 micrograms] ingested orally. The solution is tasteless.*
> *4:50 PM: no trace of any effect.*
> *5:00 PM: slight dizziness, unrest, difficulty in concentration, visual disturbances, marked desire to laugh....*

—Albert Hofmann

OVERDOSE

EXPECTING ANOTHER SHORT, "not unpleasant inebriation," Hofmann found the extremely small quantity he had ingested to be a "substantial overdose," causing a profound disruption of ordinary perception. In his journal he wrote:

> *The faces of those present appeared like grotesque colored masks; strong agitation alternating with paresis; the head, body, and extremities sometimes cold and numb; a metallic taste on the tongue; throat dry and shriveled; a feeling of suffocation; confusion alternating with a clear appreciation of the situation.*

> *I lost all control of time; space and time became more and more disorganized and I was overcome with fears that I was going crazy. The worst part of it was that I was clearly aware of my condition though I was incapable of stopping it. Occasionally I felt as being outside my body. I thought I had*

died. My ego was suspended somewhere in space and I saw
my body lying dead on the sofa. I observed and registered
clearly that my alter ego was moving around the room,
moaning.

A doctor arrived after Hofmann reached "the height
of the crisis" and found a somewhat weak pulse but
normal circulation. Six hours after he began the test of *d*-
lysergic acid diethylamide tartrate for mental effects,
Hofmann's condition improved definitely, though "the
perceptual distortions were still present. Everything seemed
to undulate and their proportions were distorted like the
reflections on a choppy water surface. Everything was
changing with unpleasant, predominantly poisonous green
and blue color tones. With closed eyes multihued,
metamorphosizing fantastic images overwhelmed me.
Especially noteworthy was the fact that sounds were
transposed into visual sensations so that from every tone
or noise a comparable colored picture was evoked, changing in form and color kaleidoscopically."

A SENSE OF WELL-BEING

FEARING HE HAD POISONED HIMSELF with a substance he
himself had made, Hofmann was particularly concerned
that he hadn't made a proper "leave-taking"
from his wife and family, who had traveled
earlier that morning to nearby Lucerne. After
a night of frightening visions, he felt relieved
the next morning and curiously rejuvenated. "What I
found further surprising about LSD was its ability to
produce such a far-reaching, powerful, inebriated condition
without leaving a hangover. Completely to the contrary,
on the day after the LSD experiment I felt myself to be
in excellent physical and mental condition...."

I had no
hangover.

"A sensation of well-being and renewed life flowed
through me. Breakfast tasted delicious and was an extraor-
dinary pleasure. When I later walked out into the garden,
in which the sun shown now after a spring rain, every-

thing glistened and sparkled in a fresh light. The world was as if newly created. All my senses vibrated in a condition of highest sensitivity that persisted for the entire day....It also appeared to me to be of great significance that I could remember the experience of LSD inebriation in every detail."

EXTREME POTENCY AND UNIQUENESS

WITH THIS EYE-OPENING, frightening experience, Hofmann entered a world largely unknown to Westerners but long familiar to tribal users of "sacred," mind-altering plants. LSD was something genuinely new in two important ways. First was the extreme potency of this compound—which figures out at 100,000-300,000 substantial doses to the ounce. Second, LSD is the first psychedelic that does not occur in nature. Mescaline had been synthesized after analysis of peyote, but it was the same drug as in the plant. LSD never existed before Hofmann synthesized it.

When his superior, Arthur Stoll, read Hofmann's report, he telephoned immediately to ask, "Are you certain that you have made no mistake in the weighing? Is the stated dose really correct?" Professor Ernst Rothlin, director of the pharmacology department at Sandoz, and two of his colleagues repeated the experiment using only a third of what Hofmann had tried. Even with this reduction, the effects were "extremely impressive and fantastic." As Hofmann has put it since, "All doubts in the statements of my report were eliminated."

Subsequent studies were carried out by Werner Stoll, the son of Arthur Stoll, involving forty-nine administrations to twenty-two people at the University of Zurich. In 1947, he published the first article on LSD's mental effects in the pages of the *Swiss Archives of Neurology*. This was followed in 1949 by his second communique on LSD to this journal, entitled "A New Hallucinatory Agent: Active in Very Small Amounts." Two further studies on clinical experiences with LSD were issued that same year.

SEEDS TAKING ROOT

OTHER DISTRIBUTION ROUTES to the general population were soon developing. From about 1957, a leak sprang up at Sandoz's Hanover, New Jersey plant. Chester Anderson, author of *The Butterfly Kid* and several other books about this period, wrote that large amounts of LSD and psilocybin with the Sandoz label were being conveyed into "beatnik" Greenwich Village and being taken by musicians, theater people, and many others living Bohemian lifestyles.

A fair amount of peyote had also become available as interest in psychedelics spread. Many people had read Huxley's *Doors of Perception,* in which he describes mystical feelings evoked by mescaline sulfate, and Wasson's *Life* magazine account of the discovery of "sacred mushrooms" and their ceremonial use in Mexico.

The newcomers attracted to LSD were not looking for a psychotic-type experience, nor were they interested in basic research. However, they also weren't taking it just for fun or to get high. The drug had acquired a mystical aura. Although it was used less solemnly and with less forethought than before, its use incorporated overtones of spiritual or artistic value. Many were using it to enhance creative behavior.

> *The drug acquired a mystical aura.*

4

MILITARY INVOLVED

SD WAS BEING STUDIED both at the Veterans Administration Hospital in Palo Alto, California, and at Stanford University. Anthropologist Gregory Bateson—who had been introduced to LSD by Dr. Harold Abramson, one of LSD's pioneers—arranged in 1959 for the poet Allen Ginsberg to take it as part of a research program that was secretly sponsored by the military. Novelist Ken Kesey also received LSD in Palo Alto, using his experiences as the basis for his *One Flew Over the Cukoo's Nest.* Kesey's further adventures with LSD are celebrated in Tom Wolfe's *The Electric Kool-Aid Acid Test.* From Palo Alto, LSD began seeping into San Francisco.

Abbie Hoffman, whose first LSD was supplied by the Army, relates how interest in the drug burgeoned along the West Coast toward the end of the 1950s. "Aldous Huxley had told me about LSD back in 1957. And I tried to get it in 1959. I stood in line in a clinic in San Francisco, after Herb Caen *Ginsberg & Kesey were among the first subjects.* had run an announcement in his column in the San Francisco Chronicle that if anybody wanted to take a new experimental drug called LSD-25, he would be paid $150 for his effort. Jesus, that emptied Berkeley! I got up about six in the morning, but I was about 1,500th in line...so I didn't get it until 1965."

CIA COVERT USE

THE CIA BECAME AWARE of LSD in the very early 1950s. That 1/100,000ths of an ounce could "derange" an individual for eight to ten hours was a matter of great

---

CIA hoped LSD could be used as a weapon.

---

concern to people there. They sought to find out more about its potential than could be gleaned from a few journal articles. They wanted to know how it could be used as a weapon, and whether it would work as a truth serum. Learning about "psychotomimetics" such as LSD became still more important to the CIA in 1951 when military intelligence reported, erroneously, that Sandoz had sent fifty million doses to the Soviets.

CIA BUYS IN

IN 1953, A MILITARY OPERATIVE in Switzerland indicated that Sandoz wanted to sell 10 kilograms—22 pounds, or about 100 million doses—on the open market. A secret coordinating committee that included CIA and Pentagon officials recommended unanimously that the CIA should buy it all for just over a quarter million dollars in order to keep it "out of the hands of the Russians or other possible buyers." CIA chief Allen Dulles approved, and soon two Agency representatives were sent to Sandoz to negotiate.

As it turned out, their informant had mistaken a milligram for a kilogram, miscalculating by a factor of a million. The president of Sandoz told the visitors that all production until then amounted to less than 40 grams, under one and a half ounces. The ergot used by Sandoz as a starting material had taken many years to find. As a result, it seemed likely that the world supply of LSD would always remain small.

Nonetheless the Swiss company indicated a willingness to step up its efforts and produce as much LSD as the CIA wished. It further agreed to keep the CIA informed about all future production, as well as requests for purchases coming in from other parts of the world.

CIA EXPERIMENTS

THE CIA ESTABLISHED a research team in the chemical division of its technical services staff. Richard Helms, then heading Clandestine Services, recommended the project in early April, 1953; a week and a half later—almost exactly a decade after Hofmann's first trip—Allen Dulles approved. The project was dubbed MKULTRA, superseding Project ARTICHOKE, and given an initial budget of $300,000. The goal:

CIA asked Eli Lilly to synthesis LSD without ergot.

"to investigate whether and how it was possible to modify an individual's behavior by covert means." Heading the group of about half a dozen was a protégé of Helms, Dr. Sidney Gottlieb, who was authorized to draw on the Agency's account.

This group was interested in determining the effects of LSD and other drugs in diverse situations. Unlike Sandoz, which was seeking therapeutic applications, the CIA was providing grants through front organizations to encourage any research. Gottlieb and his associates soon became sponsors of LSD studies conducted at a number of prestigious institutions: Boston Psychopathic Hospital, Mount Sinai Hospital, Columbia University, the Addiction Research Center of the National Institute of Mental Health, the University of Oklahoma, and the University of Rochester. "Suddenly there was a huge new market for grants in academia," wrote John Marks in his book, *The Search for the "Manchurian Candidate,"* which is the best description of these activities. Academics collaborating with the CIA in LSD investigations—some wittingly, many unwittingly—issued a multitude of articles in the scientific literature. These reports hardly reveal what a few of the "witting" were trying to find out for the CIA.

An outstanding example is Dr. Harold Abramson, a New York immunologist who apparently delighted in administering the drug to intellectuals—one instance being Frank Fremont-Smith, who later chaired one of the Josiah Macy, Jr. Foundation conferences that brought together early LSD researchers. Abramson wrote prominently about LSD in scientific publications, mainly about such things as the effect of the drug on Siamese fighting fish—they float at an angle with their noses nearly out of the water, and their color darkens—and the use of low dosages in aiding psychotherapeutic transference.

It wasn't publicly known until the late 1970s that the CIA furnished him with $85,000 in 1953 to provide—as Gottlieb put it—"operationally pertinent materials along the following lines: a) Disturbance of Memory; b) Discrediting by Aberrant Behavior; c) Alteration of Sex Patterns; d) Eliciting of Information; e) Suggestibility; f) Creation of Dependence." Abramson kept in touch with many who had begun to investigate clinical uses of LSD, reporting his findings and theirs to the CIA.

WITHOUT CONSENT

GOTTLIEB HIRED ABRAMSON and others and funded academics as a relatively inexpensive way to acquire a broad range of information about LSD and similar substances, when used in more or less ordinary settings.

The CIA also wanted information on how LSD could be used for its own special ends, information that professors were hardly likely to provide. Only a month after its establishment, the Gottlieb group set up a safehouse in Greenwich Village where people could be observed after they had been given the

Uninformed administration can be traumatic.

drug without "informed awareness." The person in charge was George White, a New York narcotics agent who had carried out experiments with *Cannabis* derivatives in search of a truth serum for the OSS, a forerunner of the CIA. The CIA paid the rent and provided White with money to hire prostitutes. Their job was to see whether individuals could be led under the influence of LSD to disclose closely-held secrets.

Desiring control of LSD as a policy objective, the CIA was worried about its dependency on a foreign supplier. In 1953, the Gottlieb group therefore approached Ell Lilly & Co., which had already been working on a process for fully synthesizing LSD. The next year Lilly's chemists made a breakthrough, manufacturing small amounts of LSD from chemicals other than ergot. An Agency memo to Allen Dulles proclaimed that the government could now buy LSD in "tonnage quantities."

CIA EXPERIMENTS RESULT IN A DEATH

EACH MEMBER OF THE GOTTLIEB group took LSD several times, and even dosed each other. Scarcely half a year after the establishment of MKULTRA came an unexpected blow that threatened to end all the goings-on. One of their university sources had told Gottlieb's group that LSD might be dangerous in some cases, mentioning a Swiss doctor who had become depressed after she took the drug and who was rumored to have committed suicide. Gottlieb had furthermore been warned twice by his superiors not to turn on outsiders. He was to see first-hand how traumatic uninformed administration could be.

The Technical Services branch of the CIA, which funded the Gottlieb group, was also paying $200,000 a year to scientists with the Army Chemical Corps at Fort Detrick for investigations relating to chemical warfare. In November 1953, Gottlieb's staff gathered with their Army associates for a three-day brainstorming retreat at an isolated lodge in the Maryland woods. During the second evening, Gottlieb passed around a glass of Cointreau which—unknown to the others—he had spiked with LSD. All but two tried the Cointreau.

Among those who partook from Gottlieb's glass was Dr. Frank Olson, a specialist in airborne delivery of chemical weapons, who came to believe that he had revealed important secrets during his subsequent LSD trip. He became depressed and was sent, accompanied by

Gottlieb's assistant, to see Abramson. Reluctantly, Olson agreed to enter a mental hospital. The night before his commitment, he crashed through a window on the tenth floor of the New York Statler-Hilton Hotel and died.

CIA GETS AWAY WITH IT

ALL CIA INVOLVEMENT with LSD was quickly covered up, only coming to light in 1976—twenty-three years later—as a result of the Rockefeller Commission's review of illegal CIA domestic activities. In 1977, Olson's family was invited to the White House for an apology, and Congress passed a bill to pay Mrs. Olson and her three children $750,000 in compensation.

Gottlieb was reprimanded by his superiors. For a short while his supply of LSD was taken from him. CIA outposts in Manila and Atsugi, Japan, were told not to use the LSD that had been shipped to them.

Richard Helms persisted in advocating that the "dirty tricks" branch of the CIA continue to experiment with LSD, and soon Gottlieb resumed distributing the drug. George White, promoted to Regional Narcotics Chief, moved his safehouse operation to San Francisco two years later, where he continued dosing people until 1966.

MORE MILITARY JOIN THE PARTY

MILITARY INTELLIGENCE in each branch of the armed services heard about LSD, and were fascinated. By the mid-1950s, they too were funding LSD studies. This secret CIA and military involvement is carefully documented by John Marks. The Chemical Warfare Service at the Army's Edgewood Arsenal stockpiled enormous quantities of LSD and other psychoactive compounds, synthesizing known psychedelics like LSD and others that may still be unknown to the outside world. On the other hand, MDMA, which since then has widely been recognized as a psychedelic agent, is identical to Edgewood's "EA [Experimental Agent]-1475."

USE IN WAR

ARMY SPOKESMEN BEGAN TALKING publicly about large-scale use of LSD in war. In contrast to the emphasis on individualized administration favored by the CIA, Army officials were showing congressmen and the press films of soldiers who were unable to march in formation after being dosed with LSD in their morning coffee. LSD was advocated as a way to conduct "humane warfare" against an enemy. Hofmann later revealed that the Army was contacting him "every two years or so" to request Sandoz's active participation in its efforts. The requests were denied.

NOTORIOUS ARMY EXPERIMENTATION

THE ARMY ENGAGED IN COVERT "field operations" overseas. A notorious example is the torture of James Thornwell, a black American soldier in France, who was suspected of having stolen classified documents in 1961. We will probably never know the full story on at least nine others, referred to as "foreign nationals," who were subjected to the Army's LSD interrogation project, operation THIRD CHANCE.

Subjects were tortured and given LSD without knowing it.

Thornwell, then twenty-two, was first exposed to extreme stress, which included beatings, solitary confinement, denial of water, food and sanitary facilities, and steady verbal abuse. After six weeks, he was given LSD without his knowledge. The interrogators threatened "to extend (his shattered) state indefinitely," according to an Army document dug up later, "even to a permanent condition of insanity."

In the late 1970s, Thornwell sued the U.S. government for $10 million; the U.S. House of Representatives approved a compromise settlement of $650,000 in 1980.

5

POP CULTURE

UST AFTER THE ELECTION OF JOHN KENNEDY to the presidency, a pediatrician of English extraction working in New York City wrote Sandoz on New York Hospital letterhead requesting a gram of LSD. A package came by return mail to Dr. John Beresford, with a bill for $285, the approximate cost of manufacture at the time. Beresford had tried other psychedelics, was impressed by the mind/body questions they posed, and was eager to test this new product. Results were somewhat surprisingly clear. He therefore gave part of his gram—over time—to a few associates, including an acquaintance known as Michael Hollingshead.

Hollingshead is important to this chronicle because he gave some of this gram to Donovan, Paul McCartney, Keith Richards, Paul Krassner, Frank Barron, Houston Smith, Paul Lee, Richard Katz, Pete La Roca, Charlie Mingus, Saul Steinberg, Timothy Leary, Richard Alpert, Ralph Metzner, Alan Watts, and many others who contributed to the coming international awareness of LSD. "There is some possibility," wrote Hollingshead later, "that my friends and I have illuminated more people than anyone else in history." His memoir bears the publisher's title, *The Man Who Turned On the World*.

With one gram Hollingshead turned on the world.

LSD CENTERS

WITH HIS PART OF GRAM "H-00047," Beresford, with Jean Houston and Michael Corner, opened an LSD foundation in Manhattan in 1962 called the Agora Scientific Trust. The impressive, valuable work carried out there is described in Robert Masters and Jean Houston's book entitled *The Varieties of Psychedelic Experience.*

That same year Myron Stolaroff and associates established another important LSD study center, the International Foundation for Advanced Study, in Menlo Park. This institution was set up to examine the effects of LSD and mescaline upon carefully selected subjects. The results from several hundred administrations were significant, especially in regard to learning enhancement and creativity.

Frank Siteman

John Beresford   Michael Hollingshead

AWARENESS EXPANDS

BY 1962, THE NUMBER OF PEOPLE who knew about LSD had increased geometrically. Some were enthusiastic about trying the drug but had no access to LSD psychotherapists, the original gate-keepers. In response to the demand for LSD, the first generation of acid chemists arose.

FIRST BUST

A NOTABLE EARLY LSD BUST was over a batch of 62,000 tablets of questionable content synthesized in 1962 by Bernard Roseman and Bernard Copely. These tabs figured in the first LSD bust, when Food and Drug Administration agents charged the two with smuggling, which they actually hadn't done. Manufacturing of LSD was then perfectly legal.

LSD MILLIONAIRE

STANLEY OWSLEY ENTERED THE TRADE after having been frustrated in his efforts to obtain pure LSD. His trademarks—"White Lightning," "Purple Haze" and others such as "Batman," "Purple Double-Domes," and "Midnight Hour"—were regarded as tabs of high quality. An enormous amount of this production was given away, yet Owsley became perhaps the first LSD millionaire. When he was captured in 1967, 200 fresh grams—a million substantial doses—were confiscated.

The first big wave of popular interest was gathering momentum. In 1962, the Gamblers issued the first record including a song about LSD. Many folk musicians were getting "cerebrally electrified." Talk of LSD spread beyond Bohemian and university circles; even Henry Luce, publisher of *Time* and *Life* magazines, and his wife tried the drug. Luce, wandering out into his garden in Arizona, heard a symphony in his head that impressed him greatly—he had previously considered himself tone-deaf. He also acquired affectionate feelings for the cacti there. This may not sound like much, but he claimed it was important personally because he previously, "had hated them."

TIMOTHY LEARY

TO CENTERSTAGE CAME Dr. Timothy Leary. Already engaged in psilocybin research at Harvard, Leary was one of those who partook of "Lot No. H-00047." He took a tablespoon and a half from Hollingshead's mayonnaise jar of LSD cut with sugar-icing—and didn't talk for five days. Richard Alpert, his close associate, "told everybody not to touch the stuff—we had just lost Timothy." When Leary came back, Alpert remembers him as saying, "Wow!"

LEARY IS TRANSFORMED

LEARY'S LSD EXPERIENCE, coming after more than a hundred psilocybin trips, changed his life. "I have never recovered from that shattering ontological confronta-

Norman Seeff

Timothy Leary

tion," he wrote later. "From the date of this session it was inevitable that we would leave Harvard...." The break was not long in coming. "LSD is more important than Harvard," proclaimed Leary in 1962. Before Timothy Leary, the academics had never quite come clean about their experimenting with LSD. Leary alone emphasized publicly that the drug was "ecstatic," "sensual," and "fun." "It gives you levity and altitude," was his explanation once, "where you see the implausibilities and you see the incongruities and the ridiculousness of what you had taken so seriously before." He gave the media a clear and emotionally charged image to transmit. Before long Leary's name was tied inextricably to the compound now known simply as LSD.

"TRAINING" EFFORTS

LEARY AND ASSOCIATES TRIED IN MANY WAYS to train people in the use of this drug, which they saw as a key to the new age. Even before leaving Harvard, they established an off-campus organization known as IFIF—the International

Federation for Internal Freedom—and laid
Live out your plans for an experiential LSD center on the
own highest beach at Zihuatanejo, Mexico. When they
vision. advertised this opportunity the next summer,
IFIF received more than 1,500 applications.

Leary requested 100 grams of LSD, about a million doses, and 25 kilograms of psilocybin, about two and a half million doses, from Sandoz, and sent a check for $10,000 as a deposit. Sandoz returned the check when Leary couldn't provide proper import licenses.

The Mexican Center lasted only a short while, because of hyped media attention after an American whom they wouldn't allow to participate caused trouble and after an unrelated murder in the vicinity. Leary and his colleagues then tried to set up an experiential center on the Caribbean island of Dominica, but their visas were canceled the day the main group arrived.

CONSCIOUSNESS WORKSHOPS

FINDING HAVEN at last on a 2,500-acre estate in Millbrook, N.Y., the remaining group announced the formation of the Castalia Foundation. Here they began turning on many influential people, as well as conducting advertised "nondrug workshops" in consciousness change. They started their *Psychedelic Review* in the summer of 1963 and traveled around the United States lecturing about LSD. They pioneered in the presentation of "light shows." Leary eventually set up a religion—the League for Spiritual Discovery. This was not intended as a mass organization, but was limited to a hundred people centered around the Millbrook estate who were dedicated to showing others how they themselves could "help recreate every man as God and every woman as Goddess." Leary emphasized that it would "not repeat the injunction classically used by religious prophets: Follow me, sign up in my flock. It imposes no dogmas except one: Live out your own highest vision."

LSD AND MUSIC

THE MONTEREY, California Pop Festival of 1963—four years before the film *Monterey Pop*—marked a new relationship between LSD and music. Many there took LSD to celebrate and enhance their appreciation of this festival. Musicians and artists soon began wide-scale experimentation with ways to perform that would complement, direct,

PSYCHEDELIC REVIEW

**Issue Number 1
SUMMER 1963
$1.50**

and heighten the effects of LSD, or present a "flash" of the experience for the uninitiated. Within a year, the Beatles were singing to everyone, "Turn off your mind, relax and float downstream. This is not dying," words taken directly from *The Psychedelic Experience*, a book issued by Leary and associates.

NOT BEATNIKS

BY THE MIDDLE OF THE 1960s, an important shift in avant-garde energies took place in San Francisco that was to reverberate powerfully throughout the Western world. This shift involved a geographical move of only a few miles—from North Beach to a vicinity near the crossing of Haight Street and Ashbury Avenue, close to Golden Gate Park. Here LSD users banded together, soon signaling the dawning of another new age.

North Beach had served for years as home ground for beatnik activities, and had become a center for cultural ferment in America. The beats generally favored stark contrasts of black and white, in their dress and in their

Every man as God and every woman as Goddess. thinking. They emphasized the role of the Artist and the Bohemian, celebrated blacks as culture heroes, and were politically active against The Bomb. Their style found expression in after-hours poetry and jazz in coffeehouses. Their taste in drugs included pot, peyote, speed, and heroin.

The Haight-Ashbury community, catalyzed by LSD, wore the colors of a rainbow and was not emphatically male dominated. It celebrated not the agonies and triumphs of the Individual Artist, but rather was "into" communal living and a new "Bay Area" style of music and dancing. Its approach was softer. If it emulated anyone, it was the tribal American Indian.

By 1966, Haight-Ashbury was rife with new energies provided by LSD—using musical groups such as the Jefferson Airplane, the Grateful Dead, Big Brother and the Holding Company, and Country Joe and the Fish; by artists such as Mouse, who with his colleagues re-established the powerful appeal once accorded posters; and by the Diggers, who gave away food and clothing. That year, the brothers Ron and Jay Thelin opened the nation's first "headshop" and helped launch the first "psychedelic newspaper," *The San Francisco Oracle.*

Ted Druck: Millbrook

The fify-one room "Big House" at Millbrook.

Less conspicuous developments took place in East Greenwich Village. The new style was evident in the low-rent centers of most large U.S. cities. The participants were mainly whites in their teens to thirties, the "baby boom" sons and daughters of the financially secure.

SECOND RENAISSANCE

AN LSD OR "FLOWER-CHILD" LIFESTYLE was encouraged through other "Be-Ins," rock music performed with light shows, dozens of psychedelic newspapers, and communal living. This proselytizing occurred throughout the U.S. and to a lesser extent in Western Europe, radiating especially from London, Hamburg, and Amsterdam.

The movement was proclaimed at the time as a Second Renaissance. Seen in retrospect, it was at the very least life-altering for millions. Some three or four years of social experimentation, touched off by mass use of LSD, can be credited with having sparked a host of liberation movements. This period changed American attitudes toward work, toward the police and the military, and toward such groups as women and gays. It began our now-established concern with consciousness-raising and personal growth.

Artifacts reflecting the creative ferment during this time are best displayed in *Psychedelic Art*, with commentary by Robert Masters, Jean Houston, and Stanley Krippner. Lester Grinspoon and James Bakalar from Harvard compiled a list of LSD's contributions—largely missing before then—to our popular language.

Turned on, straight, freak, freaked out, stoned, tripping, tripped out, spaced out, far out, flower power, ego trip, hit, into, mike, plastic [meaning "rigid"], going with the flow, laying [a] trip on someone, game-playing, mind-blowing, mind games, bringdown, energy, centering, acid, acidhead, good trip, bum trip, horror show, drop a cap or tab, karma, samsara, mantra, groovy, rapping, crash, downer, flash, scene, vibes, great white light, doing your thing, going through changes, uptight, getting into spaces, wiped out, where it's at, high, ball, zap, rush, and so on....

—*Psychedelic Art*

Poster announcing the Be-In, January 14, 1967,
in San Francisco's Golden Gate Park.

SUMMER OF LOVE

THE BIG LSD WAVE CRESTED during 1967's Summer of Love.
Wearing flowers in their hair, several hundred thousand people
came to San Francisco. Gonzo journalist Hunter S. Thompson
recalls the atmospherics of this period: "San Francisco in the
middle sixties was a very special time and place to be a part of.
Maybe it meant something. Maybe not, in the long run...but no
explanation, no mix of words or music or memories can touch
that sense of knowing that you were there and alive in that
corner of time and the world.... You could strike sparks anywhere. There was a fantastic universal sense that whatever we
were doing was right, that we were winning.... Our energy

would simply prevail. There was no point in fighting—on our side or theirs. We had all the momentum; we were riding the crest of a high and beautiful wave."

Then came "computer acid"—one hundred dots in rows of twenty by five on a sheet of blotter paper the size of a dollar bill—which was of pretty good quality, and very convenient for distribution. At about the same time arrived "Windowpane"—also known as "Clearlight"—which contained LSD inside a thin gelatin square a quarter of an inch across. Both showed improvement in potency and purity, in comparison to most blotters around, giving impetus to the flowing in of another LSD wave.

By the end of the 1970s, it was evident that a general reassessment of the earlier, massive LSD experimentation had taken place and that a less flamboyant reacquaintance with LSD had begun. The quality of the products soon available, coming from many different sources, was no longer so seriously in question. Of great importance to this resurgence of interest was the widespread home-production of psychedelic mushrooms. LSD came back into limited public discourse as a sidelight in conferences on the effects of psychoactive mushrooms.

NATURAL PSYCHEDELICS

THROUGHOUT the 1960s and early 1970s, few people actually experienced sacred mushrooms. The bulk of mushrooms examined at testing facilities

Cartoonist R. Cobb reflects the conviction that the hippy alternative is obvious and compelling.

San Francisco Chronicle

An example of visionary artwork featured in the psychedelic newspaper, *San Francisco Oracle.*

during this period were shown to be almost entirely non-psych-oactive, and many had LSD or PCP added—usually in small amounts. In 1976, successful methods for growing the *Stropharia*—often called *Psilocybe-cubensis* mushroom species were published with clearly identifying photographs. Nearly a quarter million of these instruction books and booklets were sold over the next few years, allowing great numbers of people to experience—or re-experience—psychedelic effects from a natural source.

Many who feared synthetic products because of the uncertainties of quality and identification were willing to give natural psychedelics a try. They had been used for millenia, and nothing had been charged against them in terms of chromosomal or other damage. Thanks to the gentle psychoagents in the *Stropharia cubensis* mushroom species, many people discovered or renewed an interest in LSD.

Better Living Thru Chemistry
This 1967 poster exemplifies "hippie" attitude—non-threatening
and welcoming everyone to "doing your own thing."

CHROMOSOMES

IT HAS NOW BEEN WELL ESTABLISHED that the pure LSD molecule
doesn't affect chromosomes at all. This is evident from repeated
tests made before and after administration of up to 2,000 mcg.
quantities. A summary of the first sixty-eight studies and case
reports—the bulk conducted by NIMH—can be found in the
April 30, 1971 issue of *Science* magazine. The article concludes
that "pure LSD ingested in moderate doses does not damage
chromosomes in vivo, does not cause detectable genetic damage,
and is not a teratogen or carcinogen in man."

6

BIRTH OF THE COUNTERCULTURE

THE DEVELOPMENT OF AN ALTERNATIVE CULTURE in the 1960s resulted from many influences, including the Vietnam war, the availability of psychedelic drugs, and the prosperity that enabled war babies to become flower children. Thousands and then millions of people experimented with psychedelics. Several important consequences were to flow from this widespread experimentation.

A POLITICAL ACT

TAKING A PSYCHEDELIC BECAME A POLITICAL ACT. Experimenting with marijuana, for instance, was a statement that the government's case against it was exaggerated. Benevolent experiences with marijuana led many to question authority in other areas as well. If the government misinformed people about marijuana, what about our role in the Vietnam war? What else might be in error? Use of stronger psychedelics contributed to the skepticism.

Taking psychedelics was a political act.

FEELINGS OF UNITY

PSYCHEDELIC FESTIVALS CALLED "BE-INS" were the natural outgrowth of the feelings of unity experienced when taking psychedelics, as were many efforts at communal living. Whereas previously psychedelics were usually taken by only one person, often in a clinical setting, the new emphasis was on open, uncontrolled, large-scale enjoyment of expanded consciousness.

Stephen Gaskin held his "Monday Night Class" at the San Francisco Family Dog Auditorium, which spilled over into amazing acid picnics involving hundreds of hippies on Mt. Tamalpais in Marin County, with the park rangers watching from afar through binoculars. The public was frightened at the massiveness of this movement, many fearing that some alien force was stealing its children away.

Viewed as a psychedelic Pied Piper, Alpert blames the over-exuberance of early LSD missionaries for triggering a general hysteria about psychedelics—especially Ken Kesey and the Merry Pranksters, who conducted acid tests with LSD in a punch. "We thought we had a few more years of sneaking under the wire with legitimacy before the whistle got blown. But Ken made them blow the whistle. I mean, the day after the San Jose Acid Test, the big headline in the paper was about a 'Drug Orgy.' Then the legislators had to act. Their hand had been forced."

USE AND MISUSE

THE QUESTION OF USE AND MISUSE has always been a difficult one in regard to psychedelics, and it can never be answered satisfactorily because the experience depends so much upon circumstances, attitudes, and the presence or absence of a ritual. The traditions of shamanistic use, the famous "Good Friday experiment," and the psychedelic work at Spring Grove Hospital are examples for setting up good rituals. When the psychedelic experience is seen as sacramental, as a special event to be prepared for, the results are bound to be better than if they're viewed as recreational, as a way to stave off boredom.

FOR ONLY A FEW?

TIMOTHY LEARY WENT TO THE HEART OF THIS MATTER in an essay entitled "After the Sober, Serious, Safe and Sane '70s, Let Us Welcome the Return of LSD." He restated a controversy that raged among the pioneers of the psychedelic age as to whether these substances should be reserved for use by only a few, or whether they were appropriate for "democratization, even socialization."

Leary's Apology

Summing up what he saw as the results from "seven million Americans" having used LSD, Timothy Leary concluded that our current knowledge of the brain and current patterns of LSD usage *suggest that the Huxley-Heard-Barron elitist position was ethologically correct, and that the Ginsberg-Leary activism was naively democratic. Our error in 1963 was to overestimate the effect of psychological set and environmental setting. We failed to understand the enormous genetic variation in human neurology....*

LSD and psilocybin did seem to be fool-proof intelligence-increase (I^2) drugs because our experiments were so successful! In thousands of ingestions we never had an enduring bad trip or a scandalous freak-out. Sure, there were moments of terror and confusion aloft, but confident guidance and calm ground-control navigation routinely worked. Our mistake, and it was a grave one, was that we failed to understand the aristocratic, elite, virtuous self-confidence that pervaded our group...

It was the Heisenberg Determinacy once again. We produced wonderful, insightful, funny, life-enhancing sessions because we were a highly selected group dedicated to the scientific method. We were tolerantly acceptant of ambiguity, relatively secure, good-looking, irresistibly hopeful, and romantic. So we fabricated the realities which we expected to create. We made our sessions wonderful because we were wonderful and expected nothing but wonder and merry discovery!

Psychedelic usage can be life-changing, particularly in terms of one's relationships with others. The spiritual insights achieved may make it difficult to live in the same way one has in the past. As to who Leary believed was most likely to gain from the experience is worth keeping in mind. He wrote, "Acid is not for every brain....Only the healthy, happy, wholesome, handsome, hopeful, humorous, high-velocity should seek these experiences. This elitism is totally self-determined. Unless you are self-confident, self-directed, self-selected, please abstain."

Acid is not for every brain.

ACTIVISM REDUX

SEVERAL CONVENINGS OF PSYCHEDELIC ACTIVISTS WERE INITIATED by Weston La Barre, Jonathan Ott, and R. Gordon Wasson, and their call for a re-examination of mushrooms was generalized gradually to other psychedelics, including LSD. In 1977, Hofmann and his wife Anita flew to the Olympic Peninsula in Washington state for a mushroom conference. Wasson, Hofmann, Carl Ruck, and Danny

Jeremy Bigwood

Carl Ruck, Albert Hofmann, R. Gordon Wasson, and Danny Staples at the Second International Conference on Hallucinogenic Mushrooms, held in 1977 near Port Townsend, Washington.

Staples presented evidence that the famous Eleusinian Mysteries were catalyzed by lysergic acid amides extracted from grasses on the nearby Rarian Plain.

Similar gatherings occurred in Santa Cruz, in October 1977; in San Francisco, September 1978; in Los Angeles, January 1979; in Santa Cruz, July 1981; and in Santa Barbara, March 1982.

NEW GENERATION

ANOTHER GENERATION OF YOUNG LSD CHEMISTS TOOK OVER from those who were active in the 1960s. Acid is available in myriad forms. Almost all current products contain considerably less LSD than Owsley once thought proper, but appear to be good quality. Though available in crystalline or liquid form, most LSD is still distributed on blotter paper, which is convenient but exposes the drug to possible oxidation and damage from light.

Blotters range in appearance from graph paper, containing fifty times fifty, or twenty-five hundred hits, to fancy color imprints on separated half-inch squares. These are often intricately designed, featuring a four-color Mickey Mouse as the Sorcerer's Apprentice in *Fantasia*, Rosicrucian symbols, a phoenix, a dragon, or an Eye of Horus. Some users of LSD object to the more flippant symbols, such as Plutos or Snoopys; they argue that such designs in combination with the usually low dosages encourage an LSD experience that is little more than recreational.

LSD has appeared in a hardened gel in the shape of a tiny pyramid. This is convenient for distribution, and the hardened surface reduces potential for oxidation. Tablets with LSD spread throughout offer a similar advantage in stability over blotters, one example being the "Om" tab. An appropriate direction in the packaging of LSD would be to emphasize known dosage and purity, as was the case with the original Sandoz ampules which contained one milligram per milliliter of water in a

Steve Gladstone

From left, Bonnie Golightly, Richard Alpert, Allen Ginsberg, Albert Hofmann, and Ralph Metzner in 1977 at "LSD–A Generation Later" at the University of California, Santa Cruz, where 4,000 listened to Dr. Hofmann's talk.

resealable glass container. That kind of quantitative and qualitative care has not appeared as yet.

The course of LSD history has been influenced by the establishment of several publications and institutions, including *High Times* and similar magazines, the Fitz Hugh Ludlow Memorial Library in San Francisco, NORML, or the National Organization to Reform Marijuana Laws, drug-testing facilities, and the tradition of annual Rainbow Gatherings in various parts of the U.S. Also notable are books from Stanislav Grof, Albert Hofmann, Carlos Castaneda, Timothy Leary, and many others.

Dosage is down, causing less potential for panic, along with less spectacular results. The number of people interested went on the rise. Charlie Haas summed up the change in his "Notes on the Acid Renaissance" in *New West* magazine:

Notes on the Acid Renaissance

*LSD—the scariest and most tantalizing thing you can buy
without a prescription, the white hope for instant psychotherapy that became a CIA toy and a bazooka in the
Bohemian arsenal, the portable Lourdes that oiled the
transition of American youth from Elvis to Elvish and made
all those honor students start dressing funny and printing up
those unreadable purple-and-aqua posters—that LSD—is as
nationally popular now as it was ten years ago, despite the
fact that the same media which then could speak of nothing
else are now virtually silent on the subject. Among people
who swallow it or sell it, or who monitor its use from the
vantage point of drug-abuse counseling, there is some sporting
disagreement as to whether acid has been enjoying a renaissance for about two years or never went away in the first
place, with the former view in the majority. But there is a
consensus on at least two points: The bad trips and mental
casualties that made such hot copy in the '60s seem to have
diminished radically, and the volume of acid changing hands
suggests that there are actually more users now than there
were a decade ago....*

—Charlie Haas
New West Magazine

7

HYSTERIA

ITH THE FIRST LSD WAVE came a wave of establishment panic. The federal ban on LSD and related
drugs was the first bill proposed by President Johnson
in 1967. A clash between traditional American mores and the
values adopted by users of Hofmann's crystal had been on its
way ever since Harvard University sent Alpert and Leary packing
over the issue.

The media hurried the conflict to its moment of crisis; for
a while it seemed there wasn't a nationally distributed magazine
that didn't have an LSD article, usually sensational. *Time* was
the first to jump in with a series of
articles appearing in late 1965 and early
1966 in its Psychiatry section. These
articles railed against LSD—with dire

*Confusion was great;
knowledge was small.*

warnings about hordes of "acid heads," some of whom were
taking "walloping overdoses."

Time declared that the "disease" was striking everywhere: "By
best estimates, 10,000 students in the University of California
system have tried LSD, though not all have suffered detectable
ill effects. No one can guess how many more self-styled 'acid
heads' there are among oddball cult groups...."

Dr. Houston Smith of MIT wasn't far from the mark when
he told an LSD conference in 1966 that the confusion about
this drug was so great and our knowledge about it so small
"that there is no hope of telling the truth about it at this
point." All efforts to arrive at a deliberate and informed evaluation of the drug were swept aside by the headlines of that year.

In the Headlines

On March 26th, 1966 Timothy Leary was arrested in Laredo after less than half an ounce of marijuana was found on his daughter. The sentence was thirty years. Leary was suddenly transformed into the LSD movement's first martyr.

On April 6th, a five-year-old girl in Brooklyn swallowed a sugar cube impregnated with LSD that her uncle had left in the family refrigerator. She was rushed to the hospital where her stomach was pumped. She got the scare of her life through this procedure, and remained on the critical list for two days. Published reports of her being examined later indicated that she made a full recovery.

On April 11th, Stephen Kessler, a thirty-year-old ex-medical student, was charged with the murder of his mother-in-law, having stabbed her 105 times. When taken in, he muttered, "What happened? Man, I've been flying for three days on LSD. Did I kill my wife? Did I rape anybody?" At the Brooklyn police station, he kept insisting, "I'm high, I'm really high," and when asked if he were "high" on drugs, he replied, "Only on LSD".

On April 16th, G. Gordon Liddy, then assistant prosecuting attorney in Dutchess County, N.Y., broke into national prominence by leading a raid on Leary's Millbrook estate, where, at a cost of $60 per weekend, nondrug techniques were being used to teach people how to get "high."

Liddy since has said that he liked Leary from the moment he first set eyes on him at 2 am, but that he was "acting under orders." A small amount of marijuana was found in the room of a visiting journalist, and Rosemary Woodruff, who was to become Leary's wife, was held in jail for a month for refusing to testify before a grand jury about activities on the estate.

The headlines prompted an appetite for still more coverage. Special interviews with district attorneys, college presidents, narcotics agents, doctors, biochemists, and others who might be considered authorities appeared, creating an atmosphere of national emergency.

MORE DANGEROUS THAN HEROIN

THE CHAIRMAN OF THE New York County Medical Society's Subcommittee on Narcotics Addiction declared that LSD is "more dangerous than heroin." The FDA and Federal Narcotics Bureau launched new "drug education" programs. Three Senate subcommittees investigated LSD use. Bills that made possession of LSD and other psychedelic drugs a felony were introduced into state legislatures throughout the nation. New York State Assembly Speaker Anthony J. Travia, pushing legislation that called for a minimum sentence of seven years, declared that he would defer public hearings on the law until after it passed because "the problem is so urgent."

One to two million American tripped.

Walter Winchell issued an item reading: "Warning to LSD Users: You may go blind." Bill Trent, writing in the Canadian *Evening Telegram* about an architect's serious and successful attempt to solve a design problem by taking LSD, titled his story "The Demented World of Kyo Izumi." The mass-market *Confidential Flash* asserted in a full-page cover headline: "LSD Kills Sex Drive Forever." *The Police Gazette* reprinted a report from *The Journal of the American Medical Association* with a new title, "LSD and Sex Madness."

PROGRAM CUTS

IN ONE OF THE SENATE LSD HEARINGS, Senator Robert Kennedy repeatedly asked why the studies conducted by the National Institute of Mental Health, which had been thought so valuable a month earlier, "no longer were considered so?" It was a question almost nobody wanted to hear or have answered. In short order, existing programs were drastically cut back. Before long, there were new, tighter regulations. Any investigator who had ever experienced the drug personally was now forbidden to conduct LSD research of any kind whatsoever.

DRIVEN UNDERGROUND

AND YET, AS THE CONSUMERS UNION'S BOOK *Licit and Illicit Drugs* notes, "by shutting off the relative trickle of Sandoz LSD into informal channels, Congress and the Food and Drug Administration had unwittingly opened the sluices to a veritable LSD flood. By 1970 it was estimated that between 1,000,000 and 2,000,000 Americans had taken an LSD trip." The Consumers Union noted further that driving the drug and its users underground augmented certain of its hazards.

Hazards of Underground Use

Increased expectations of adverse effects
Unknown dosages
Contamination
Adulteration
Mistaken attribution
Side effects of law enforcement
Lack of supervision
Mishandling of panic reactions
Misinterpretation of reactions
Flashbacks
Preexisting pathology
Unwitting use

CHROMOSOME BREAKAGE

DR. MAIMON COHEN, a geneticist from Buffalo, N.Y., made an announcement in 1967 that significantly prejudiced the public's view of LSD. Returning from a visit to the Haight-Ashbury area, Cohen decided to examine chromosomes from a fifty-seven-year-old man who had been given LSD on four occasions during a fifteen-year hospitalization. The patient was found to have more chromosomal breaks than usual.

Cohen poured LSD into a test tube containing human cells and observed damage to the chromosomes. Later it was pointed out that similar results could be achieved with the same amount of milk, and that Cohen's patient had received regular treatments of Librium and Thorazine, now proven chromosome-breakers. Nonetheless, on

Leary's chromosomes showed no significant aberrattion.

Apologia for Timothy Leary
Michael Horowitz

the basis of his examination of a single patient and his cell-spilling experiment, Cohen published his conclusions in *Science.* By evening, the charge that LSD could break chromosomes was in all the nation's media.

Shortly thereafter, two doctors in Portland, Oregon, reported that they had found an excess of chromosomal breaks in users of street acid. The chart they provided revealed that extra breakage occurred only among users of acid who were also users of amphetamine, which has since been established as a chromosome-breaker. Once again the papers had a field day. A full-page ad for a *McCall's* article on LSD featured a baby broken into parts. Ironically, the article itself cast doubts on the charge of chromosome damage.

Retractions of mistaken opinions and findings about the use and effects of LSD are quiet and very rare, and so it was in regard to the chromosome charge. Though studies subsequently conducted by the National Institute of Mental Health and others disproved the allegation. Timothy Leary's chromosomes were examined. Hermann Lisco, M.D. of the clinical team reported "Timothy Leary, much of our surprise, showed, in 200 cells, only two with chromosome aberration, one in each cell. This finding is about as spectacular as must be the amount of LSD that he probably has taken in the past 8 years. I am at loss to understand or explain this negative finding." In fact, other drugs have been found to be chromosome-breakers while LSD is not. Nonetheless, the myth lives on.

A Case In Question

As a footnote it should be pointed out that at the trial of Stephen Kessler—the "Mad LSD Slayer"—it was learned that he had taken LSD five times in minimal doses, 10-50 mcgs., between the summer of 1964 and March 1966, a month before the murder of his mother-in-law. Other drugs, however, may have been influential in the slaying. The New York Times reported that "the defendant made no mention of having taken LSD just before the killing of Mrs. Cooper, but said that on April 8, a Saturday, 'I felt funny. I had an indescribable feeling and took one-and-a-half grains of pentabarbital' and could recall nothing more until after the murder, the following Monday...."

The New York Post reported that "both doctors...told the jury of eleven men and one woman that Kessler had told them he had drunk three quarts of lab alcohol, cut with water, and taken more sleeping pills on the days in question...."

Ebb and Resurgence

The National Institute on Drug Abuse, or NIDA, issued a National Survey on Drug Abuse in 1977, based on a sampling of 4,594 people. The report estimated that about ten million Americans—6 percent of the population over the age of twelve—had by then used a strong psychedelic, mostly LSD, with somewhat over a million falling into the category of "regular users."

Peak Years

The peak years of psychedelic use were from 1965 to 1968, followed by a substantial decline in LSD use. Many were frightened by the chromosome-damage charge or by

experience with adulterated or badly made
LSD. Others were put off by the overwhelming nature of "high-dose tripping," or
by its illegal status, fearing that the need to
act furtively would interfere with and badly
taint the LSD experience. Large numbers of
previous users turned to meditation to get high.

*Stark got some
35 million
doses from
Europe.*

LSD OUTLAWED

OCTOBER 16, 1966 IS AN IMPORTANT DATE in psychedelic
history. It is the day when California outlawed LSD, an
action later repeated by the federal government. It is also
the date of the first "Be-ins," which occurred both in
San Francisco and New York City. Soon after, Sandoz—the
only legitimate source of LSD and psilocybin—stopped
supplying these chemical agents to American investigators.
Sandoz turned over the remainder of its stockpile in its
New Jersey facility to the National Institute of Mental
Health, which in turn soon curtailed research programs
using psychedelic drugs in human subjects from more
than a hundred down to a grand total of six. The
chances of anyone getting "pharmaceutically pure" LSD
rapidly dwindled.

ALTERNATIVES

DOM—ALSO CALLED STP—WAS INTRODUCED to the counterculture in 1967, but soon was withdrawn amid controversy
over excessive dosages and impurities. It still appeared on
rare occasions, sometimes sold as STP but often disguised
by a less stigmatized name. "Orange Wedge" LSD appeared in early 1968, in strong dosages and available
internationally. It was followed in early 1969 by another
massive psychedelic production effort—the "Sunshine" trip.
In both cases, allegations sprang up that these products
had been adulterated with speed, STP, strychnine, and
other contaminents.

ARRESTS

SOME OF THE LEADING UNDERGROUND CHEMISTS had been
arrested. The LSD available was generally weaker and less
pure, though there were exceptions—tabs known as
"Mighty Quinn," "Blue Cheer," "Pink Swirls," and the
red, white, and blue "Peace Sign." "Sunshine" acid—an
orange tablet less than a quarter of an inch across—was
the first large
operation after
LSD posses-
sion was made
illegal. Tim
Scully, a
prominent
second-genera-
tion chemist,
made some
but said that
most "Sun-
shine" came
by way of   Drug bust at Tompkins Square,
Ronald Stark,   New York City
an extraordi-
nary mysterious fellow who brought approximately
thirty-five million doses over from Europe.

East Village Other

LSD use reached its lowest ebb in the early 1970s
and manufacturing shrank to a small scale. Those seeking
LSD could find pink, blue, and purple microdots, but
very little else.

8

TRIPPING

LSD CAN BE SWALLOWED, taken on the tongue—producing perhaps the most rapid effects—or absorbed through the skin, particularly with DMSO. It has been absorbed in the form of eye-drops and baked in cookies or cake frosting. It has been ingested by almost every means except smoking. LSD taken by mouth has effects that occur almost as rapidly as by intramuscular injection.

Anywhere from twenty minutes to an hour after being swallowed, this chemical—which often produces an immediate "metallic taste"—may cause one or a few of the following physical sensations: slight chill, dilation of the pupils, vague physical unease concentrated in the muscles or throat, tenseness, queasy stomach, tingling in the extremities, drowsiness. When a novice is asked, "How do you feel?" the answer is likely to be "I don't know" or "Different." If asked about feeling all right, the experiencer will probably not be very sure.

Much is beyond verbal description.

The physical sensations which accompany LSD are usually minor. Often they cannot accurately be likened to sensations ever felt before. As time passes, such physical effects usually disappear. In a few instances, however, they persist throughout much of the experience.

DOSAGE

THE ACTION OF LSD IS DIFFICULT TO CLASSIFY because it isn't specific, like aspirin or Miltown. More confusing, it also has variable effects at different dosages. Dosages estimated comparable by weight often result in widely fluctuating reactions in different animals. Furthermore, within a given species there may be idiosyncratic responses—even when subjects are all of the same age, weight and sex. Yet dosage can be one of the most important determining factors.

Most users are affected by dosages above about 20 mcg. Amounts just above this produce effects somewhat like a long-lasting "hash high"; Hofmann's initial trip is a fair example. From about 75 mcg. up to about 125 mcg., the amount usually taken, LSD can emphasize internal phenomena, although it is frequently used at this level for interpersonal matters, problem-solving, or for the enhancement of sensations—for example, at a rock concert. A heavy dose—on the order of 200-250 mcg.—produces a predominantly interior, revelatory experience. Higher doses tend to intensify the trip rather than lengthen it; above 400-500 mcg., there seems to be a saturation point, beyond which increases make little difference.

Higher doses increase intensity rather than lengthen the trip.

EXPERIENCES VARY

THE EFFECT OF A PARTICULAR DOSAGE varies greatly from person to person. Body weight is certainly a factor, but time of day, use of other drugs, mental set, and physical setting all play important roles. Generally, 100-250 mcg. is considered a good initial dose, and this can be adjusted at the time of the next session to suit the individual.

Another consideration is the extent of other drug usage. Chronic alcoholics and heavy narcotics users who are on maintenance doses usually need about twice the ordinary amount of LSD to arrive at comparable effects.

Narcotics users who have been free of opiates for less than a year are often hypersensitive, and their dosage must be adjusted with great care. Pretreatment with a minor tranquilizer may be indicated.

INJECTION

LSD IS A CURIOUS CHEMICAL. When given by injection, it disappears rapidly from the blood. It can be observed when tagged with Carbon 14 in all the tissues, particularly the liver, spleen, kidneys, and adrenal glands. The concentration found in the brain is lower than in any other organ—being only about 0.01 percent of the administered dose. Sidney Cohen, in *The Beyond Within,* has estimated that an average dose results in only some 3,700,000 molecules of LSD—about 2/100ths of a microgram—crossing the blood-brain barrier to interact with the billions of cells that make up the average-size brain—"and then for only a very few minutes."

ORALLY ACTIVATED

LSD IS HIGHLY ACTIVE when administered orally, absorbed through mucous membranes or through the skin, and is almost completely absorbed by the gastrointestinal tract. Concentrations in the organs reach peak values after only ten to fifteen minutes; then they decrease very rapidly. An exception to this rapid decrease has been observed in studies with mice, which show

Acid can be absorbed through the skin.

activity in the small intestine increasing over a period of a few hours. Some 80 percent of ingested LSD is excreted via the liver, bile system, and intestinal tract, with only about 8 percent appearing in urine. After two hours, only 1 to 10 percent is still present in the form of unchanged LSD; the rest consists of water-soluble metabolites—such as 2-oxo-2, 3-dihydro-LSD—which do not possess any LSD-type influence on the central nervous system.

PEAKING

PSYCHIC EFFECTS OF LSD reach their peak about one to three hours following ingestion, when much of the substance has disappeared from the body's major organs, including the brain, though measurable amounts persist in the blood and brain for about eight hours.

ALARMING SYMPTOMS

IT IS NOT AT ALL UNCOMMON to find users experiencing alarming symptoms or sensations, especially during the early phases—the impression of giving birth, melting into the floor, being born, and so on. A few feel that their heart has stopped beating or that their lungs aren't operating regularly any more. These symptoms should be taken as a sign of altered perception. No one is on record, for instance, as ever having suffered an LSD-provoked heart attack. However odd it may seem at the time, the body carries on without problems.

The body carries on without problems.

MEDICAL HAZARDS

FOR THOSE CONCERNED ABOUT immediate medical hazards in ingesting LSD, short references might be in order. Abram Hoffer has estimated, on the basis of animal studies, that the half-lethal human dose—meaning half would die, a standard measure for drugs—would be about 14,000 mcg. But one person who took 40 mg., or 40,000 mcg., survived. In the only case of death reportedly caused by overdose—written about in the *Journal of the Kentucky Medical Association*—the quantity of LSD in the blood indicated that 320 mg., or 320,000 mcg., had been injected intravenously.

Worries about whether the body under ordinary amounts of LSD will operate all right are only mental illusions. Whatever the mental effects induced by this drug, a physician would notice only physiological changes.

Physiological Changes

Slight increase in blood pressure
Slight increase in pulse rate
Increase in salivation
Increase lactation in women
Slight rise in temperature
Dilation of the pupils

Pupil dilation occurs more markedly as a result of oral administration than from injection. Stanislov Grof, perhaps the most seasoned psychedelic guide ever, thought pupil dilation was the only invariable effect of LSD for quite a while, but then observed an instance in which this oscillated with "pinning." LSD doesn't affect respiration, though anticipation of such an effect may, on a few occasions, cause small alterations.

COURSE OF TRIP

SOME PSYCHEDELICS CAUSE NAUSEA OR GIDDINESS upon ingestion. The usual course is to reach an initial "high plateau" shortly after the onset of action. This plateau constitutes the first quarter or third of the experience. After that, there is often a build-up of intensity, to the "peak" of the experience, usually occurring about halfway through the session.

Recall of the trip is usually sharp and detailed.

During the second half of the experience, the effects gradually diminish, although mental stimulation may last in a more subdued fashion for some time. Memory of the experience is generally sharp and detailed, and physical after-effects are minimal. Feelings of elation are common, and can continue for a day or longer afterwards.

DURATION

WHATEVER ITS DURATION, a psychedelic experience most often widens the scope of awareness. One is transported internally to what Huxley called "The Other World"—a locale experienced spiritually, esthetical, and intellectually. The environment perceived during ordinary states of mind isn't altered, but the perception of it is. This perceptual transformation of the external world is temporary, but the insights can be significant and lasting.

Psychedelic recognition can be compared crudely to seeing a glass as "half empty" and then seeing it "half full." A CIA agent's description to John Marks illustrates such a switch-over in awareness. As Marks recounts it, he began "...seeing all the colors of the rainbow growing out of cracks in the sidewalk. He had always disliked cracks as signs of imperfection, but suddenly the cracks became natural stress lines that measured the vibrations of the universe. He saw people with blemished faces, which he had previously found slightly repulsive. 'I had a change of values about faces,' he says. 'Hooked noses or crooked teeth would become beautiful for that person. Something had turned loose in me, and all I had done was shift my attitude. Reality hadn't changed, but I had. That was all the difference in the world between seeing something ugly and seeing truth and beauty.'"

Oscar Janiger.

HEIGHTENED AWARENESS

GENERALLY, AN INITIATE'S FIRST COMMENT focuses on heightened awareness of internal and external sensations and on alterations in "unalterable reality." Early LSD researcher Dr. Oscar Janiger listed these as "an unusual wealth of associations and images, the sharpening of color perception, the synesthesias, the remarkable attention to detail, the accessibility of past impressions and memories, the heightened emotional excitement, the sense of direct and intrinsic awareness, and the propensity for the environment 'to compose itself' into perfect tableaus and harmonious compositions...."

MULTILEVEL THINKING

THE LINEAR NATURE OF ORDINARY THOUGHT is replaced via a psychedelic with a more intuitive, holistic, and "holographic" approach to understanding reality. Thoughts occur simultaneously on several levels—a dramatic demonstration of the mind's ability to resonate at different frequencies. Investigators compare the logic of this "other world" to that of dreams and other functions often associated with the right hemisphere of the brain.

Unalterable reality alters.

DREAM STATE

THE PSYCHEDELIC EXPERIENCE can be likened to being in a dream state where one is wide awake and remembering. That right hemispheric brain functions are amplified is consistent with experiential reports. People tell of enhanced sensitivity to rhythm, as well as new appreciations of music and dance. Robert Masters and Jean Houston theorize that the rhythmic aspect marks a progression into deeper "stages." In their *The Varieties of Psychedelic Experience,* they described four stages of deepening awareness.

EXPANDED SENSATIONS

GENERALLY SPEAKING, THE PSYCHEDELICS touch a spiritual core, have exhibited physical healing qualities, have been used ritualistically, facilitate creative problem-solving, and change the sense of time and spatial relationships. They are neither addictive nor toxic. Because their most significant action is mental, and, thus, fairly non-specific,

Andrew Weil has characterized a psychedelic as being like "an especially active placebo," meaning that one's response depends very much on one's expectations. Art Kleps, much experienced with psychedelics, was once asked, "What are the side-effects of LSD?" He said, forthrightly, "There are nothing but side-effects."

IMPACT

VIRTUALLY EVERYONE WHO HAS TAKEN a powerful psychedelic comes away impressed. Psychologist Ralph Metzner observed over a period of years that people awakened by psychedelics to the myriad possibilities for human consciousness often go on to pursue other ways and methods of increasing awareness. Osmond, writing in the *Annals of the New York Society of Medicine*, described the awe that is a frequent sustained effect. "Most subjects find the experience valuable, some find it frightening, and many say that it is uniquely lovely. All, from [anthropologist J.S.] Slotkin's unsophisticated Indians to men of great learning, agree that much of it is beyond verbal description. Our subjects, who include many who have drunk deep of life, including authors, artists, a junior cabinet minister, scientists, a hero, philosophers, and businessmen, are nearly all in agreement in this respect. For myself, my experiences with these substances have been the most strange, most awesome, and among the most beautiful things in a varied and fortunate life. These are not escapes from but enlargements, burgeonings of reality...."

Expections drive the trip.

Elimination of Limitations

I had begun to do hatha yoga. I was experimenting with being a vegetarian and I had never done any body-work before, and, for me, yoga was very discouraging. I found that there were a number of postures that not only could I not get in, but there seemed to be no hope of getting in. There was one in particular that was really a great stumbling block to me, and that was "The Plough." I would lie on the floor and get my feet over my head, and when my toes were about a foot from the floor I would get an excruciating pain in my neck. I felt so bad I could hardly get out of the position I was in. I tried for at least four or five weeks to work at that every day, but there was no progress. I made a little progress at first, and then hit what seemed to be

Jeremy Bigwood

Andrew Weil

an absolute limit defined by this pain in my neck. I was really on the verge of giving up. I thought that I was too old—I think I must have been twenty-eight then—and stiff. I thought I had waited too long to do yoga; it was just an impossibility.

Well, we all took acid on this perfect day. There were puffy clouds, butterflies, and all the usual things on a wonderful spring day. I was feeling so good that at some point I thought, "Well, gee, I ought to try doing some yoga postures." And I lay down, and I tried The Plough. When I thought I had about a foot to go, my toes touched the ground—and I couldn't believe it! I raised my legs and lowered them, and kept raising them and lowering them, and not only was there no pain in my neck, it felt great!

*I burst out laughing, it was so wonderful—and suddenly I had
this feeling that nothing was impossible, that all the limits I
had imagined just weren't there suddenly. And, "If I could do
that, why couldn't I do all these other things that I never
thought I could do?" In fact, I began doing some of them.*

*The next day, still elated from this experience, I tried to get
into The Plough. And, a foot from the floor, there was that
excruciating pain in my neck again. But there was a difference. I knew I could do it now, and the fact that I knew it
was possible motivated me to keep working at it. If I had not
had that experience, I would have given up. There was no
reason to think that I would have continued in that direction.
Having had that experience changed what that meant for me.*

—Andrew Weil

9

EXPANDED CONSCIOUSNESS

THE 1960s PSYCHEDELIC MOVEMENT coincided with a general recovery of the religious impulse—especially interest in Eastern religions. A new flexibility in religious belief and spirituality came about at a time when influences such as existentialism had convinced many that "God is dead." Psychologist Stanley Krippner has suggested that the psychedelics were "the single most important factor in bringing back dedication to this country."

> Many gave up eating meat.

A sense of harmony spread with the use of psychedelics, along with a new appreciation of non-violence. However, these religious feelings weren't organized; they occurred spontaneously within individuals and were accepted largely as recognitions common to people who had seen beyond ordinary states of consciousness. Many became vegetarians after an eight- or ten-hour experience made them feel that they couldn't eat flesh any more.

Religious Origins

When we consider the origin of the mythologies and cults related to drug plants, we should surely ask ourselves which, after all, was more likely to happen first: the spontaneously generated idea of an afterlife in which the disembodied soul, liberated from the restrictions of time and space, experiences eternal bliss, or the accidental discovery of hallucinogenic plants that give a sense of euphoria, dislocate the center of consciousness, and distort time and space, making them balloon outward in greatly expanded vistas?

Perhaps the old theories are right, but we have to remember that the drug plants were there, waiting to give men a new idea based on a new experience. The experience might have had, I should think, an almost explosive effect on the largely dormant minds of men, causing them to think of things they had never thought of before. This, if you like, is divine revelation....

Looking at the matter coldly, unintoxicated and unentranced, I am willing to prophesy that fifty theobotanists working for fifty years would make the current theories concerning the origins of much mythology and theology as out-of-date as pre-Copernican astronomy.

—Mary Bernard
The American Scholar

At the core, LSD enables the users to transcend ordinary reality and feel religious effects. Huxley described the experience with a term from Catholic theology—"gratuitous grace." He wrote Father Thomas Merton about similarities perceived by one user to spontaneous mystical experience: "A friend of mine, saved from alcoholism, during the last fatal phase of the disease, by a spontaneous theophany, which changed his life as completely as St. Paul's was changed by his theophany on the road to Damascus, has taken lysergic acid two or three times and affirms that his experience under the drug is identical with the spontaneous experience which changed his life—the only difference being that the spontaneous experience did not last so long as the chemically induced one."

It had an almost explosive effect on dormant minds.

Philosopher and Zen master Alan Watts had a bad first impression, characterizing his LSD experience as "mysticism with water wings." During two later experiments conducted by associates of the Langley-Porter Clinic in San Francisco, he quickly changed his mind. He reported "I was amazed and somewhat embarrassed to find myself going through states of consciousness that corresponded precisely with every description of major mystical experiences that I had ever read. Furthermore, they exceeded both in depth and in a peculiar quality of unexpectedness the three 'natural and spontaneous' experiences of this kind that had happened to me in previous years."

PROFOUND EFFECT

THE RELIGIOUS ASPECT OF LSD ingestion registered strongly among the group at Harvard running the Psilocybin Research Project. Shortly after the project had begun, Michael Hollingshead showed up with a jar filled with LSD. It was given to third-year Ph.D. students in behaviorism. Hollingshead reflected on that small class of students and their instructors.

The Harvard Resonance

Al Cohen runs the Meher Baba group. He got his Ph.D. in behaviorism.

Richard Alpert already had his Ph.D. He's a Hindu saint.

Tim Leary already had his Ph.D. He became the "High Priest."

Ralph Metzner got his Ph.D. He is now running healing work and wholistic therapeutic groups in San Francisco and Berkeley, the total opposite of behaviorism. Ralph accepts that within each person there's a spiritual entity which can be moved if it's once awakened and allowed not only to see but also to be.

Gunther Weil is now the director of the Media Center of the University of Massachusetts, but he's also been running the Gurdjieff group in Boston. He is closely identified with the Gurdjieffian work. He has put out records, he has tried to create art movies, he's lectured on the acculturation of the psychedelic experience.

Al Alschuler was at Harvard in the School of Education. He has moved away from strict behaviorism into creative educational techniques, but through the system.

Paul Lee was Paul Tillich's right-hand man. And he had a very profound experience. He's now teaching herbs in Santa Cruz.

Rolf von Eckartsberg was in Philadelphia, running the Open House System, where certain houses are always open to ex-prison inmates.

Hollingshead concluded that for these people LSD was instrumental in realization of the importance of their religious nature. He said that "to use Aldous Huxley's expression, 'the doors of perception' were opened, and they saw inside the house—this house of many mansions which is also the Self. And then the doors closed at midnight and they were back in the old humdrum again—but vouchsaved a glimpse of the other. And then, bit by bit, they began to discover Eastern writings, the *Tao Te Ching*, the *I Ching*, the Vedas, the Upanishads, Sufi masters, various forms of music that are designed for people who are in the house to dance. And they began to move off into different areas, which accounts for why they are where they are now."

Many will have religious experiences.

Houston Smith, Professor of Philosophy at MIT, similarly described this most important aspect of psychedelics. He said that "...given the right set and setting, the drugs can induce religious experiences indistinguishable from ones that occur spontaneously. Nor need set and setting be exceptional. The way the statistics are currently running, it looks as if from one-fourth to one-third of the general population will have religious experiences if they take the drugs under naturalistic conditions, meaning by this conditions in which the researcher supports the subject but doesn't try to influence the direction his experience will take. Among subjects who have strong religious inclinations to begin with, the proportion of those having religious experiences jumps to three-quarters. If they take them in settings which are religious too, the ratio soars to nine out of ten."

Smith has given a useful definition of "a religious experience," calling it an experience that elicits from the experiencer a centered response, a response from the core of his or her being. "As his being includes thoughts, feelings, and will...a religious experience triggers in the experiencer a triple movement: of the mind in belief, of the emotions in awe, and of the will in obedience. A

religious experience is awesome, con-
vinces the experiencer that its noetic
disclosures are true, and lays upon him
obligations he acknowledges as binding."

Belief, awe and
obendience of will.

In various LSD studies, episodes of a religious nature
have often been manifested even when the intent of the
study had nothing to do with religious consciousness.
"Cure for dipsomania," William James once said, "is
religiomania," a proposition confirmed in the LSD alcoholism studies.

For the 206 psychedelic sessions guided or observed
by Masters and Houston—112 with LSD—the statistical
breakdown shown below, rounded to the nearest percent-
age, indicates the type and frequency of religious images
that arose among their subjects.

Religious Imagery

Religious imagery	96%
Religious architecture	91%
Religious art	43%
Religious symbols	34%
Mandalas	26%
Religious figures	58%
Devils or demons	49%
Angels	7%
Miraculous and numinous visions	60%
Cosmological imagery	14%
Religious Rituals	
Contemporary religous rites	8%
Contemporary Oriental rites	10%
Ancient religious rites	67%
Primitive rites	31%

The Masters and Houston report on mystical experiences is especially interesting because they have taken
pains to be more exacting than most in terms of religious
criteria. In their *The Varieties of Psychedelic Experience*, they
certify only one subject reaching the profoundest depth
and only six as attaining the "introvertive mystical" experi-

ence. About the latter, they comment that "It is of interest to observe that those few subjects who attain to this level of mystical apprehension have in the course of their lives either actively sought the mystical experience in meditation and other spiritual disciplines or have for many years demonstrated a considerable interest in integral levels of consciousness. It should also be noted that all of these subjects were over forty years of age, were of superior intelligence, and were well-adjusted and creative personalities."

When the historical scarcity of mysticism is kept in mind, these limited claims by Masters and Houston are all the more impressive. They may yet substantiate the comment from Ram Dass' guru that religion would come to America by way of a pill.

Dosage is a primary factor in the emergence of religious impulses. Lesser amounts generally have lesser effects, although small doses on occasion have induced psychically powerful results.

SPIRITUAL CATALYST

LSD PIONEER WALTER HOUSTON CLARK believes psychedelics are "catalysts" to feelings, understandings, and thinking. He pointed out that the psychedelic adds nothing to our consciousness, but it brings to the surface many parts of our consciousness that had been lying dormant most of our lives. Clark gathered questionnaires about the nature of their experiences from 140 subjects who had used psychedelics. He noted that there wasn't a single one of those responding who didn't mention at least one—and most mentioned several—of the characteristics in "the universal core" of mysticism, as compiled by a leading religious scholar.

Everything is alright.

Clark concluded "that the typical person, wherever he's found, turns out to be a mystic when you go right down to the bottom of his personality. What I'm saying is that all of us here in this room are potential mystics. As William James said in his chapter on mysticism, 'Given the appropriate stimuli, mysticism will come to the surface.'"

Huxley had a similar point of view. After writing about how use of psychedelics had deepened his feeling for the spiritual, he received a letter from Thomas Merton, the Trappist monk and noted poet, questioning the validity of drug-induced mystical experiences. Merton asked about distinctions that might be drawn between mystical and aesthetic aspects.

Mystical or Aesthetic?

There are those whose experience seems to be much more than aesthetic and may be labeled as pre-mystical, or even, I believe, mystical. I have taken mescaline twice and lysergic acid three or four times. My first experience was mainly aesthetic. Later experiences were of another nature and helped me to understand many of the obscure utterances to be found in the writings of the mystics, Christian and Oriental. An unspeakable sense of gratitude for the privilege of being born into this universe. "Gratitude is heaven itself," says Blake— and I know now exactly what he was talking about. A transcendence of the ordinary subject-object relationship. A transcendence of the fear of death. A sense of solidarity with the world and its spiritual principle and the conviction that, in spite of pain, evil, and the rest, everything is somehow all right....

Finally, an understanding, not intellectual, but in some sort total, an understanding with the entire organism, of the affirmation that God is Love. The experiences are transient, of course; but the memory of them, and the inchoate revivals of them which tend to recur spontaneously or during meditation, continue to exercise a profound effect upon one's mind.... There is a feeling—I speak from personal experience and from word-of-mouth reports given me by others—that the experience is so transcendently important that it is in no circumstances a thing to be entered upon light-heartedly or for enjoyment. In some respects, it is not enjoyable, for it entails a temporary death of the ego, a going-beyond.

—Aldous Huxley
Moksha

NOT ALL TRIPS CREATED EQUAL

SOME HAVE CRITICIZED HUXLEY'S VIEWS, pointing out that most people don't have the intellectual and imaginative resources that he brought to this experience. They claim Huxley was atypical. Clark's work, on the other hand, indicates that most people do have experiences along similar lines. What a particular individual makes of the experience is influenced by that person's knowledge, religious feeling, willingness to accept new perceptions as valid, circumstances under which the psychedelic was taken, and the amount of attention subsequently paid to the insights or feelings aroused.

10

TRIP GUIDES

LTHOUGH THIS BOOK ISN'T DESIGNED AS A SESSION GUIDE for tripping, it is appropriate here to provide some background on minimizing tight moments that may develop. The management of a session and the role of "guides" are discussed in Masters and Houston's *The Varieties of Psychedelic Experience*; in Leary, Metzner, and Alpert's *The Psychedelic Experience*; and in Cohen and Alpert's *LSD*.

John Beresford, a psychiatrist who has had much experience with psychedelics since the early 1960s, outlines a basic strategy. He emphasizes that confrontation is precisely what should be avoided when a person who has taken LSD shows signs of agitation or depression or in some other way is manifesting resistance to the natural flow of the experience. "What the person helping can do then is search for and suggest an image or idea which complements the image or idea which acted as the springboard of resistance. The resistance is undone and the normal flow of the session can proceed."

Trip Guide Should Be Honest

You are not, in this situation, dealing with a six-year-old child, who can easily be put off or led down the garden path. The ego at bay is a mobilized ego, alert to all danger, suspicious of your every move and word. Always assume that the tripper can "see right through you," no matter how bizarre the behavior. The guide should be honest. If you honestly think distraction is

called for, then say so. For example the guide might say,
"Well, if questions like that are bothering you, why not look
at some of these pictures instead?" Don't pretend a sudden
interest in something you are not really interested in at all. As
for saying, "Try not to think about it" or something of the
sort, well, try not to think of a purple cow yourself and see
how much luck you have.

Let's come right out with it. Unless you are enlightened, don't
bother trying to guide Ivory Sessions—sit by if requested to do
so, but make no pretense of being anything more than a
servant, 'ground control' or whatever the hell you want to call
it. The fact of the matter is that fakery is impossible in this
situation anyway; there are no standards; there is no third
party, no precedents, no law. It all depends, and it depends
on nothing constructible. Circumstances, and circumstances
only.

—Art Kleps
The Boo Hoo Bible

TRIP GUIDE DO'S AND DON'TS

IN *LSD—THE PROBLEM-SOLVING PSYCHEDELIC*, Bonnie Golightly
and I compiled a list of do's and don't's for psychedelic
trips.

TRIPPER IS IN CONTROL

UNDER THE INFLUENCE OF SUCH SUBSTANCES, the tripper is
not simply adrift, a tourist cast off at the mercy of the
elements and in the grip of forces that cannot be influenced. The tripper is yet in control and can change
directions. Because of the overwhelming nature of what
occurs, however, this may not be easy to remember.
Under the influence of a psychedelic, the tripper can
function normally and can also alter the experience.

This should be fully grasped before taking this type of
drug. Once into a session, the tripper should take time
out and practice reversing sensations. Water may taste like

wine just by thinking it so. A light object can be made to feel heavy, or another's glistening tears can be turned into a dry-eyed expression of joy. When sufficiently skilled, the tripper will be able to select hallucinations at will.

PREPARE FOR TAKE-OFF

FOR THE INITIATE, SOME DIFFICULTY MAY BE ENCOUNTERED in take-off, since the transition is comparable to a jet thrust. Care should therefore be taken to reduce rigidity and awkwardness. The best approach for entering inner space gently is made with the aid of a fluid, not-too-structured selection of music and simple breathing exercises, or possibly a massage, since a tense, tight attitude may grow out of waiting for something to happen.

GO WITH NEGATIVE STATES

DURING THE EIGHT OR TEN HOURS OF ALTERED REALITY under the influence of most psychedelics, much that is shocking or distasteful may occur within the tripper, especially unpleasant fantasies of a physical nature. Cardiac specialists, as well as other doctors, often direct their heightened psychedelic sensitivity to their bodies and witness in surgical detail the actions of internal organs. These physical scrutinies

Avoid confrontation if tripper is agitated or depressed.

also can preoccupy the layperson, of course, and birth experiences—being born or giving birth—are within the ordinary line of psychedelic events. Disorientation with regard to time may terrorize even the most valiant.

Many frightening hallucinations are subjective experiences with little basis in everyday fact. If the tripper wants them to go away, the best remedy is to dispense with the natural impulse to fight them. Going with them or giving one's self over disperses the unwanted vision and the screen is cleared for something else. Facing terrifying psychedelic events may call for courage and stamina in early sessions.

BOOSTING THE EXPERIENCE

IF RESISTANCE REMAINS HIGH, the experience may become repetitious, leading up to a crucial point but without a breakthrough. The tripper can vacillate—hot and cold, back and forth, endlessly affixed to the same treadmill. He or she cannot make decisions, and has been through all this many times before. In such instances, *boosting* may be called for. An additional dosage is usually enough to break the set and move the tripper off his or her plateau.

Dr. Duncan Blewett gives the rationale. He says that if you don't give a large enough dose of the drug, a person gets into a sort of interim position, with one foot in the camp of the usual frame of reference and the other in the camp of unhabitual perception. The person finds it impossible to make a break between these two.

Change the subject.

But if a large enough dose of the drug is used, so that the person is propelled rapidly out of the old context and cannot maintain the self-context as previously, then—rather than becoming more uncomfortable as you would think—he or she becomes much more comfortable and able to accept as valid this new and novel way of seeing the world.

A reason for the occasional vortex-like recurrence of the same material seems to lie in the fact that drug effects come in waves, and if the tripper is allowed to persist in one area too long, he or she may be caught in an undertow. The favored method for breaking through this hang-up is to change the subject matter completely— with the intention of returning to it later if it seems worthwhile.

If the recurrent material is deliberately brought up again after some time has passed, the subconscious will have had a chance to devise other approaches and the insight level will probably be more acute. A good technique in such instances, borrowed from hypnosis, is to suggest that in a specified length of time the tripper will return to the problem and then be able to resolve it.

RECOGNIZE PHYSICAL SYMPTOMS

THE DEVELOPMENT OF PHYSICAL SYMPTOMS—such as coldness, nausea, pressure on the spine, restlessness, tingling, tremors, or "a pain in the kidneys"—is often the body's way of evading psychedelic effects. With peyote, and to a lesser extent with sacred mushrooms or Morning Glory seeds, these effects may be attributed to the drug, but with LSD and most other synthetics such symptoms are most frequently a sign of resistance. The guide should in such cases recognize these symptoms as an indication that the drug is about to take effect, and should reassure the tripper that these physical symptoms will soon pass, with the psychedelic experience taking their place.

REACTING TO VERBAL STIMULI

ANOTHER EVASION OF THE FULL PSYCHEDELIC EXPERIENCE may involve over-intellectualizing what happens and talking on and on throughout the session. Because language depends upon familiar ways of thinking, reliance on words keeps much that is non-verbal from developing and restricts the psychedelic experience. To carry on a lengthy conversation confines psychedelia even further, since the tripper when questioned or spoken to is somewhere "out in orbit" and must then come back and touch down before replying.

Reassure the tripper.

For the average person, a period of verbalization may not develop into a problem, but a rigidly defensive person, on the other hand, may use words to avoid the experience, and as time passes may become increasingly desperate, or even aggressive, reacting with hostility towards the guide. A variety of menacing motivations may be imputed to the guide. In such a situation the guide should refuse these various ploys, gently reminding the tripper what he or she is there for.

PHYSICAL COMFORT

IF TERROR GRIPS THE TRIPPER continuously during the
session, physical comforting may lend the needed reassur-
ance. This is a delicate matter unless the guide is certain
that the tripper will accept the gesture. Because attendant
psychedelic distortions may seem too vile or alien to be
shared, the tripper who has lodged in a crevasse can most
successfully be brought out, if other means have not been
satisfactory, by the guide's taking her into his own arms
and soothing the frightened tripper.

COUNTER-DIVERSION

IF REVERSING DISTURBING HALLUCINATORY MATERIAL has not
dispelled anxiety, counter-diversion should be attempted.
The tripper should be encouraged to try some appropriate
physical activity such as dancing, keeping time to music,
playing the piano, or even gardening! Taking deep breaths
and paying attention to the lungs as they expand and
contract is quite effective. Such diversionary efforts will in
all probability become the new focus of attention.

EXTRA RESOURCES

THE SKILLED GUIDE ALWAYS HAS EXTRA RESOURCES up the
sleeve or is capable of fast, imaginative thinking. One
example, which can serve as a pattern for the latter,
occurred when a tripper decided she was made of metal
and was unable to move. "Oh, you're the friendly robot
in that TV show," the guide remarked genially, and as
the tripper was familiar with the program referred to, she
immediately "recognized herself" and began moving gaily
in a deliberate parody of an automaton's gyrations.

Leary had an amusing and instructive episode to
recount along these lines. He described an electronics
engineer who had taken psilocybin and was reacting with
great anxiety. As he told it, his traveling companion was
unable to calm him down. The psychologist in charge
happened to be in the bathroom. He called to his wife,
who was drying the dishes in the kitchen, "Straighten him

out, will you?" She dried her hands and went into the living room. The distressed engineer cried out, "I want my wife!" and she put her arms around him, murmuring, "Your wife is a river, a river, a river!" "Ah!" he said more quietly. "I want my mother!" "Your mother is a river, a river, a river!" "Ah, yes," sighed the engineer, and gave up his fight, and drifted off happily, and the psychologist's wife went back to her dishes.

UNPLEASANT HALLUCINATIONS

PINPOINTING THE SOURCE OF AN UNPLEASANT HALLUCINATION can eliminate it rapidly. One tripper, for instance, convinced that the house was on fire, said he could actually see his charred limbs in the ruins. The guide showed him a burned-out candle in an ashtray, still smoking because the wax had been set afire by cigarette butts. Another person was able to deal with distasteful psychic material when told that he was merely a visitor passing through a slum and that a better neighborhood would soon emerge.

This, too, will pass.

GAME-PLAYING

CRISES DO SOMETIMES ARISE even in well-planned sessions. If the tripper is unable to cope with them in a sober manner, the guide may suggest "game-playing." The tripper should be instructed to think of himself or herself as a versatile actor who must portray a character in a serious role, stand aside, and let the play begin.

GETTING HOME

IF THE TRIPPER HAS INSISTED UPON TAKING A STROLL through heavy traffic, wants to drive a car, or undertakes some other ill-advised pursuit, and if the guide has been outwitted or lost contact, the tripper should remind himself or herself that what is happening is due to the psychedelic taken and that its effects will, in time, wear off. Finding the way home is not an impossible feat, and the tripper should try to recall, step by step, how it was done the day before. Since evaluating distance may be difficult, it is important to obey all traffic signals rigorously in crossing streets—taking a cue from the surge of the crowd. Any inclinations towards bizarre behavior should be curbed, bearing in mind that the mission is simply to get home.

If the tripper has been driving a car, upon realization of the situation it's important to park as soon as possible, and take a cab, a bus, or proceed on foot. Although the user may not believe it, most people will have no idea of his or her condition, either through their own preoccupations or the simple fact that it is not always easy to detect psyche-delic drug behavior.

BUMMERS INFREQUENT

IN POINT OF FACT, runaway and out-of-control sessions are extremely unusual. Once a psychedelic experience has been completed, the carry-over depends on where the stepping stones have been placed or if the desired bridge has been reached. Ideally, time should be allowed for relaxation in so-called normal reality to let the subconscious integrate its new insights. This is the time to put the psychic house in order, to speculate about what has been resolved, and what remains to be resolved.

DRAWBACKS

MOST PEOPLE WHO HAVE USED PSYCHEDELICS claim that the effects from these substances on their lives have been beneficial. Many, in fact, state that they have been influen-tial in producing the most meaningful and positive experi-ences of their lives. On the other hand, a small number of people who have used psychedelics have had what they consider to be long-term negative effects. In the days when these drugs were taken with less awareness of the psychedelic experience's potentials, there were undoubtedly drug abuse tragedies. Much of the bad press for psychedelic drugs originated from these occurrences. The illegal status of LSD, psilocybin, and MDA came about as a result of the dangers inherent in self-experimentation during the 1960s.

ABUSE

A VARIETY OF PSYCHEDELIC SUBSTANCES continue to be widely used throughout our society, even though it is usually illegal to buy, sell, or even possess them. Although this author believes that their dangers have been vastly exaggerated—and are much less than the dangers of alcohol—abuse of these substances can and has occurred. Almost all of this can be characterized as involving unintelligent use.

Set and setting should be chosen with care.

Because alterations in consciousness produced in psychedelic states can possibly lead to impairment, care in choosing the circumstances, dosage, quality of drugs, companionship, and related matters should always be exercised. Thoughtless and reckless use of these compounds is a violation of their positive, indeed sacred, characteristics.

FOCUS ON THE POSITIVE

THE BEST PSYCHEDELIC EXPERIENCES ARE LIFE-CHANGING and life-enhancing. Attention paid to these matters will help bring the time when psychedelics will be more widely appreciated in our society for their medical, therapeutic, creative, religious, insightful, and relationship-enhancing capabilities.

II

CHEMISTRY

L SD-25 IS A CRYSTALLINE MOLECULE that shares, along with many other psychedelics, a two-ring indole nucleus—composed of one atom of nitrogen, eight of carbon, and seven of hydrogen—in its chemical structure. This basic structure is common to the short-acting tryptamines, ibogaine, psilocybin, harmaline, and several

LSD-25 is structurally similar to serotonin.

other psychedelics, and it bears considerable resemblance to the chemical structure of serotonin and dopamine, neurotransmitters that carry electrical impulses across synapses in the brain. Mescaline and MDA-like compounds contain only one of these rings. Nitrous oxide (N_2O) and the THCs in marijuana have considerably different chemical structures.

On top of the indolic nucleus, there are two additional rings in the structure of the LSD molecule. These are typical of the LSD family of chemicals. To synthesize LSD and its analogs, one has to obtain the preformed lysergic acid "skeleton" first and then manipulate its chemistry through quite difficult processes. Such is not the case with the one- and two-ring psychedelic compounds, which can be synthesized more readily and altered to a much greater extent.

SEROTONIN

LYSERGIC ACID, usually appearing as a metabolic product of the fungus *Claviceps purpurea* which grows on rye or barley, has an unusual chemical structure with what might be considered two asymmetric centers. Dependence of pharmacological action on the asymmetry of such compounds has been widely observed. Researchers have shown that psychedelic agents such as LSD interact with serotonin in synapses throughout the brain. Related drugs that are not psychedelic almost always lack such action.

DERIVATIVES

THROUGH THE SYSTEMATIC PRODUCTION UNDERTAKEN by Sandoz, a great many lysergic acid derivatives have been created and studied. Originally produced for medicinal purposes, most of these derivatives were re-examined after discovery of LSD's psychoactive effects. Some are psychically inactive, while others have varying psychoactive potentials. The most powerful is LSD-25.

Among the many known lysergic acid amides, a slight change in the four-ring structure has considerable consequences in terms of psychic effects. For example, LSD-25 turns a beam of polarized light clockwise; this is represented by the *d* for *dextro* at the beginning of its chemical

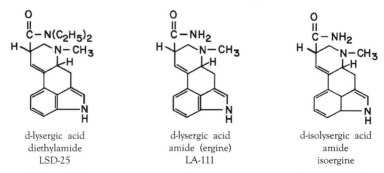

| d-lysergic acid diethylamide LSD-25 | d-lysergic acid amide (ergine) LA-111 | d-isolysergic acid amide isoergine |

LSD and the two major psychoactive agents produced in baby Hawaiian Woodroses and some Morning Glories.

N-acetyl-d-lysergic acid
diesthylamide (ALD-52)

2-bromo-d-lysergic acid
diesthylamide (BOL-148)

name. The *l-* or levo-rotary form, its mirror image, turns such a beam counterclockwise and has virtually no psychoactive effect.

Comparing the structure of LSD-25 to that of the two most active ingredients in related botanicals—the baby Hawaiian woodrose and certain Morning Glories—you'll see that these sources of LSD-like effects have different chemical structures.

LA-111 and isoergine, which were synthesized in the laboratory before they were known to occur in nature, are significant members of the LSD family. Others have such names as MLD-41, ALD-52, OML-632, LAE-32, BOL-148, MLA-74, ALA-10, LPD-824, LSM-775, DAM-57, LME, LMP, LAMP, and LEP. Of these, the acetylated, or ALD-52, and methylated, or MLD-41, analogs are the next most potent to LSD, possibly because they are quickly converted to LSD upon ingestion. Four others have about a third of LSD's strength, four about a tenth, with the others being much milder.

ALD-52 is the LSD analog that's been most often represented as acid on the psychedelic market in the last few years. "Sunshine" was allegedly ALD-52, though this has been disputed. It has slightly over 90 percent of LSD's potency and is transformed into LSD-25 upon contact with water. The resulting trip is generally said to be smoother than one with LSD-25.

A SINGLE ATOM

BOL-148 IS OF SPECIAL INTEREST because it played a considerable role in psychedelic history. BOL-148 differs from LSD-25 by a single bromine atom, which renders it inactive in terms of mental function. Yet it is capable of producing more anti-serotonin activity than LSD, and it also produces some cross-tolerance with LSD. This compound seems to contradict the simple model that the effects of psychedelics are mediated by serotonin.

The fact that it blocks or is cross-tolerant with LSD was one reason for the spread of interest in LSD as a psychotomimetic. The theory was that if psychosis had a chemical cause, and a similarly cross-tolerant substance could be found, then it would nullify psychosis just as BOL-148 nullifies the psychoactivity of LSD-25.

It is still possible that serotonin and dopamine have something to do with LSD's effects, but after decades of investigation of this compound, there's still no clear and accepted explanation for LSD's action. Speculating on the mystery surrounding the psychoactive agent he discovered, Hofmann wrote, "It is perhaps no coincidence but of deeper biological significance that of the four possible isomers of LSD, only one, which corresponds to natural lysergic acid, causes pronounced mental effects. Evidently the mental functions of the human organism, like its bodily functions, are particularly sensitive to those substances which possess the same configurations as naturally occurring compounds of the vegetable kingdom."

> *A slight change in structure has considerable consequences.*

CROSS-TOLERANCE

LSD IS GENERALLY CONSIDERED CROSS-TOLERANT WITH MESCALINE but not with psilocybin—meaning that use of LSD a day before taking mescaline will reduce the impact of the mescaline; less tolerance develops if the order of the compounds is reversed.

LSD *is cross-tolerant*
with mescaline
but not psilocybin.

It is well established that LSD is cross-tolerance with itself—self-limiting, in the sense that if a second dose is taken a day later the effects will be considerably diminished. This tolerance endures significantly for three days and does not fully dissipate for a week. Abram Hoffer has remarked that LSD is its own greatest enemy. This feature acts as a control on human abuse of this drug.

IMPURITY

THE UNDERGROUND CHEMISTS WENT TO WORK. The first underground lab to attract public attention belonged to two partners, Bernard Roseman and Bernard Copely, who were arrested in 1962 for smuggling 62,000 doses of LSD because of a story they told to misdirect attention from the fact that they themselves had made this. Production of LSD at this time was still legal. The disturbing part about Roseman's account of this affair—in his book *LSD: The Age of Mind*—was his mention that their LSD turned into a blackish, slimy material. He tried it anyway and was impressed by the effects. So the two of them packaged it for sale. The purity of psychedelics on the black market as been an issue ever since.

The first massive manufacturing and distributing operation had come into being in 1965—Stanley Owsley's marvelous tabs. Owsley came from a background of interest in amphetamine and questions as to whether he liked to add speed to the product were raised. Bruce Eisner, who has written much about the question of psychedelic purity, interviewed Owsley's lab assistant, Tim Scully, and believes that speed was never added.

PURITY IS QUESTIONED

DOUBTS ABOUT THE PURITY OF UNDERGROUND PRODUCTS were common by the 1970s—and for good reason. There were weak blotters of LSD, requiring four or five to get a buzz. At about this time, nearly a hundred drug analysis organizations, the most prominent being PharmChem in Palo Alto, examined the quality of underground psychedelic products. What they found was not reassuring. Quality control was almost non-existent.

PharmChem's Analysis of Samples

Of 405 samples said to be LSD, 91.6% were as alleged, 3.4% had no drug at all, 3% were actually DOM, PCP and others, and 2% had DOM, PCP and methamphetamine in addition to LSD.

Of 127 samples said to be marijuana, 89.7% were as alleged, 6.3% had no drug at all, 1.6% was nicotine, and 2.4% had PCP and cocaine in addition to marijuana.

Of 64 samples said to be THC, none were as alleged, 95.3% were PCP, and the rest were LSD and other substances.

Of 185 samples said to be mescaline, 17.3% were as alleged, 7.6% had no drug at all, 61.6% were LSD, 11.4% were LSD + PCP, and there were three that were PCP and two others as well.

A single sample of DMT was as alleged.

Of 59 samples said to be MDA, 71.2% were as alleged, with the rest (28.8%) composed of DOB, DOM, 2,5-DMA, PMA, PCP and LSD + PCP.

A single sample said to be MMDA was found to be LSD.

A single sample of ibogaine was as alleged.

Of 33 samples said to be PCP, 84.9% were as alleged, 12.1% had no drug at all, 3% were marijuana.

If marijuana products are excluded, just over 55 percent of so-called "psychedelics" tested out as claimed— 501 out of 906 samples. More than 9 percent contained no psychoactive substance at all and 34.5 percent were assayed as some entirely different mind-altering chemical. Although many of these samples may have been sent in for testing because there was already some question about their content, this rundown indicates a serious problem with the purity of black market psychedelics from that era.

MISREPRESENTATION

THE EARLY 1970S WAS THE WORST PERIOD OF MISREPRESENTATION. Siva Sankar recorded findings that were even worse when better analytical equipment was used. Marshman and Gibbins tested 519 samples of street drugs for which the vendor's claimed composition was available. Of the samples alleged to be LSD, 44% contained LSD with *two* or more contaminants, or even were mixtures of intermediate chemicals resulting from unsuccessful attempts to synthesize LSD. None of the drugs alleged to be mescaline contained mescaline. Lundberg, Gupta, and Montgomery analyzed several alleged street drugs, mostly from the California area. Of 96 samples sold as psilocybin, only five contained psilocybin. The rest were either LSD or mixtures of LSD and phencyclidine.

PURITY PARANOIA

IT'S UNFORTUNATE THAT UNDERGROUND MANUFACTURING and distribution of psychedelics developed this way. The purity of a complex chemical is difficult to test, and doubts about the purity of an untested chemical can create paranoia, multiplied easily while in a psychedelic state. Furthermore, an impure dose may well encourage fundamental misinterpretations by the novice as to the nature of the psychedelic experience.

All the results I have ever seen indicates that Sunshine, as an example of a suspect psychedelic, was pure LSD-25. The PharmChem listings show virtually all the acid they examined to have been pure, though the matter of

Purity of black market acid is questionable.

contaminants may not have been examined very thoroughly. It was mescaline and psilocybin that were generally revealed to be misrepresented. This situation has since improved, but there is still good cause for being wary.

While most attention has focused on purity to account for the bummers experienced by many using black market acid, it should be noted that the psychedelic molecules are delicate and should be handled gently in transport. Also, most oxidize fairly easily and should be kept away from light, heat, and water.

12

THE MIND

PSYCHEDELICS HAVE BROUGHT US CLOSER to an understanding of the human mind, as is evidenced by new directions in formal studies of the brain. Krippner has remarked that the main impact of psychedelics from a scientific point of view was to get people interested in research into consciousness—not only with psychedelics, "but with sleep, dreams, biofeedback, hypnosis, meditation, etc. Many of the very prominent consciousness researchers today, though few will admit it, were turned on to this whole experience by their early acid trips back in the 1960s."

Impact on Consciousness Research

I think it would be no exaggeration to compare the discovery of LSD, and the use of LSD, by such pioneers as Dr. [Stanislav] Grof, whom you heard last night, to the Copernican revolution, the Darwinian revolution, and the Freudian revolution.

The Copernican revolution took the human being's planet out of the center of the universe and out of the center of its own solar system and put it on the periphery. The Darwinian revolution placed the human being in direct descent from lower animals. The Freudian revolution pointed out that much of human motivation is unconscious, rather than conscious. Human beings were still holding on to that little bit of conscious motivation that they had until Albert Hofmann came along with LSD, suggesting to us that what little conscious motivation we have is chemical in nature and that it can be influenced very radically by chemicals.

*This was premature, because within the last few years there
have been many experiments with endorphans and other
neural transmitters which support this view. The chemical
basis of behavior, of memory, of cognition, and of perception
is now taken for granted more than it was back at that time.*
                                              —Stanley Krippner

THE BRAIN

IMPRESSIVE BREAKTHROUGHS HAVE BEEN MADE in mapping
receptor-sites for chemicals entering the brain, in photo-
graphing neural activity, and in improving analytical
equipment. There has been evidence confirming that
several psychedelics are normally present in people's heads.
Harmala alkaloids appear in the pineal gland, possibly in
greater concentrations among yogis. DMT has been located in the brain and in cerebrospinal fluid.

NEUROTRANSMITTERS

MANY OF THE SUBSTANCES OUTLAWED by drug legislation are
actually important neurotransmitters. Shulgin commented
on the federal prohibitions against peyote which proscribe
every compound of this plant. He said that "if this were
pushed into a point of legal absurdity, since dopamine is
a compound of the plant, and since it's a mandatory
neurotransmitter in our normal functions, it would mean
in a very humorous way we would possibly all be possess-
ors and carriers of a Schedule I drug in our normal,
healthy state."

A related finding from other analyses is that opium-
like substances are concentrated about twenty times more
than normal in the milk of mammals. Because such
compounds appear in lettuce and many of the grasses
that cows commonly graze upon, some nursing babies
must be starting life stoned.

Along with greater sophistication about the many roles
played by psychoactive compounds in people's lives and
the possibility of exposure to a wider variety of

psychedelics, psychic explorers in the future will also be beneficiaries of techniques that aim at realizing the peaks of the psychedelic experience through nondrug means, and/or are designed to enhance the productiveness of sessions.

Bruce Eisner, writing about such contemporary research, sketched some examples. He says, "We see such practices as Stan Grof placing a blindfold on the experiencer in a quiet room, putting on music, and telling him or her to go with the flow, and Salvador Roquet, who takes groups of twenty or more and bombards them with light, sound, and other means of sensory overload. John Lilly tells us that a sensory isolation tank is best, while Jean Millay would take her dose connected to a biofeedback device. And then there is Jay Hippie, merging with the light on a secluded beach."

LSD produces slight changes in the EEG, usually with decreased amplitude and increased frequency of brainwaves. Generally, there is a decrease in the alpha rhythm—though, in some cases, there is an increase. Many chemical changes occur in the brain—most of them in the midbrain, which regulates awareness and modulates emotional responsiveness. Recent attention has focused on substantial concentrations found in the brain-stem and in the dopamine receptor system, both responsible for more complex experiences.

There are natural psychedelics in the brain.

Hoffer and Osmond's *The Hallucinogens* discusses quite a number of reactions that can be seen regularly when LSD affects the mind's functions. No one really knows, however, which of these alterations are most important, because all occur simultaneously. Much of the metabolizing of LSD takes place in the liver, where peyote also lodges. Perhaps it's as the Egyptians used to think: the liver is indeed the seat of the soul.

SPECULATIVE

OUR UNDERSTANDING OF HOW LSD works physiologically and neurologically is still rudimentary, at best speculative. By the beginning of the 1970s, the most intensively examined hypothesis dealing with this interface of mind and body—regarding the displacement of serotonin at the synapses—came to be regarded as a red herring. Other theories, such as those emphasizing specific receptor sites, have not really been verified.

Brimblecombe and Pinder summarize the controversies in their book, *Hallucinogenic Agents*. "Most of the evidence which has emerged since 1966 lends support to the mode of action of LSD proposed that year by Freedman and Aghajanian, that is that interactions with the 5-HT [serotonin] receptor are the primary action of the drug and that the observed changes in metabolism of brain amines are secondary phenomena. Other biochemical changes attributed to the action of hallucinogens, particularly LSD, such as the effects on brain pseudocholinesterase levels are so contradictory that they appear to offer little insight into the mode of action of the drugs Nevertheless, a large number of questions remain unanswered. It is still not clear whether LSD is acting as an agonist or as an antagonist, neither is it clear whether the drug has direct or indirect presynaptic actions, and, most important of all, the ways in which the drug-receptor interaction and the biochemical changes are translated into neurological and behavioural phenomena are very uncertain."

BRAIN HEMISPHERES

ONE DISCOVERY THAT MAY SEEM PARTICULARLY RELEVANT is the "complete reversal of amplitude laterality," described by Goldstein, Stolzfus, and associates in 1972 after they made chronograms of the electrical activity of left and right occipital EEGs of right-handed volunteers before and after administration of several psychedelics. They found a "progressive narrowing of inter-hemispheric EEG amplitude differences with eventually complete reversal (to the right) of their relationships."

In simpler language, data processing in the brain's cerebral cortex was preferentially shifted under the influence of LSD from the more analytical left hemisphere to the visuo-spatial right hemisphere. This seems an economic and

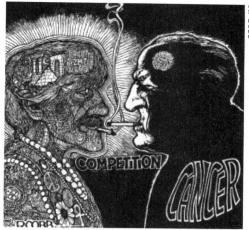

R. Cobb

Psychedelic or Tobacco?

fairly satisfactory explanation of how a psychedelic like LSD increases the scope of the mind, brings artistic, creative, rhythmic, and problem-solving abilities to the fore, and evokes phenomena that Freud referred to as manifestations of the unconscious.

One often hears that much of the brain is usually dormant. Depending on dosage, LSD may increase mental power perhaps by activating the visuo-spatial centers. In this sense, LSD and other psychedelics could be considered deliberate and unconscious agents of the right lobe. For a full discussion of the implications of this theory, consult Roland Fischer's "Cartography of Inner Space" in the Drug Abuse Council, Inc.'s 1975 book entitled *Altered States of Consciousness*.

MENTAL EFFECTS

IF THE EXPERIENCE IS ALL IT IS SAID TO BE, how can anyone go "through this kind of thing without turning into a terrorized blob of babbling jelly?" Kleps wondered and then added, "The state is difficult to describe because it is akin to mystical experience, which is...ineffable!"

"How to describe it!" exclaimed Henri Michaux, the French poet and painter, speaking of the psychedelic experience. "It would require a picturesque style which I do not possess, made up of surprises, of nonsense, of sudden flashes, of bounds and rebounds, an unstable style, tobogganing and prankish."

However, in many ways LSD can also be viewed as a relaxant, as a means to mental calm and to centering. It frequently puts the user in a serene state of mind and at ease. Many users describe it as bringing on the feeling, perhaps for the first time, that they are home.

If that sounds like a contradiction, so be it. The states of consciousness brought about are often paradoxical. This might be expected from a catalyst that channels the brain from a dualistic to a unitary way of looking at things. Here's what Allen Ginsberg had to say when *Playboy* magazine asked what LSD does.

Tripping

What does a trip feel like? A creeping sensation comes over your body, a change in the planetary nature of your mammal eyeballs and hearing orifices. Then comes realization that you're a spirit inhabiting a vast animal body containing giant apertures, holes, circulatory

Steve Gladstone

systems, interior canals and mysterious back alleys of the mind. Any one of these back alleys can be explored for a long, long way, like going back into recollections of childhood or going forward into the future, imagining all sorts of changes in the body, in the mind or in the world outside, inventing imaginary universes or recalling ones that existed, like Egypt.

Allen Ginsberg

Then you realize that all these exist in your mind simultaneously. Slowly you approach the mysterious feeling that if all these histories and universes exist in your mind at the same time, then what about this one you're really in—or think you are? Does that also exist only in your mind? Then comes a realization that it does exist only in your mind; the mind created it. Then you begin to wonder, Who is this mind? At the height of the acid experience, you realize that your mind's the same mind that's always existed in all people at all times in all places: This is the Great Mind—the very mind men call God. Then comes a fascinating suspicion: Is this mind what they call God or what they used to call the Devil? Here's where a bum trip may begin—if you decide it's a demonic Creator. You get hung up wondering whether he should exist or not.

> The states of consciousness may be paradoxical.

To get off that train of thought: You might open your eyes and see you're sitting on a sofa in a living room with green plants flowering on the mantelpiece. Outside the window, wind is moving through the street in all of its forms—people walking under windy trees—all in one rhythm.

The more you observe the synchronous, animal, sentient details around you, the more you realize that everything is alive. You become aware that there's a plant with giant cellular leaves hanging over the fireplace, like a huge unnoticed creature, and you might feel a sudden, sympathetic and intimate relationship with that poor big leaf, wondering: What kind of an experience of bending and falling down over the fireplace has that stalk-blossom been having for several weeks now?

You realize that everything alive is experiencing on its own level a suchness existence as enormous to it as your existence is to you. Suddenly you get sympathetic, and feel a dear brotherly-sisterly relationship to all these selves. And humorous, for your own life experiences are no more or less absurd or

weird than the life experience of that plant; you realize that
you and plant are both here together in this strange existence
where trees in the sunroom are blossoming and pawing
toward the sky. Finally you find out that if you play them
music, they grow better.

So, the widening area of consciousness on acid consists in
your becoming aware of what's going on inside your own head

———————— cosmos—all those corridors leading into dreams,
Who is this   memories, fantasies—and also what's happening
mind?   outside you. But if you go deep enough inside,
                you may find yourself confronted with the final
problem: Is this all a dream-nature? Great ancient question:
What is this existence we're in? Who are we? Then can come
what Timothy Leary terms the "clear light" experience or, as
they call it in South America, "looking into the eyes of the
Veiled Lady"—looking to see who it is, doing or being all this.
What's the self-nature of it all? This is the part of the acid
experience that's supposed to be indescribable, and I'm not
sure I've had the proper experience to describe it.

—Allen Ginsberg

13

PSYCHOTHERAPY

IX YEARS after Hofmann's discovery, LSD was taken to Los Angeles by Nicholas Bercel, a psychiatrist specializing in the electroencephalograph, or EEG, who had been handed some casually by the younger Stoll with a request that he try it. LSD was requested and received through the mail at Boston's Psychopathic Hospital, where it was first given to Dr. Robert Hyde, the Assistant Director. After swallowing 100 mcg., he became paranoiac but claimed that there was no effect and that the hospital had been cheated. He even insisted on making his hospital rounds. An associate commenting later said, "That was not Dr. Hyde's normal behavior; he is a very pleasant man."

The psychiatrists A.K. Busch and W.C. Johnson also sent for LSD, looking for "a good delirient" for use in therapy. They thought LSD "might shake up things," as Busch later remarked. By August 1950, they were discussing the drug's role as a possible aid in psychotherapy in an American journal, *Diseases of the Nervous System*. They wrote, "We believe that

It may offer a means to access chornically withdrawn patients.

LSD-25 is a drug which induces a controllable toxic state within the nervous system, that reactivates anxiety and fear with apparently just enough euphoria to permit recall of the provoking experiences. It does this without the sluggishness or speech difficulties so frequently encountered during IST [Insulin Shock Therapy] and following

ECT [Electroconvulsive Therapy]. On the basis of the preliminary investigation, LSD-25 may offer a means for more readily gaining access to the chronically withdrawn patients. It may also serve as a tool for shortening psychotherapy. We hope further investigation justifies our present impression."

SANDOZ LABS

THE HISTORY OF LSD UNTIL CURBS WERE PLACED upon further experimentation, can be seen in microcosm in Hofmann's first two experiences of the drug. Initially there was keen interest and optimism. As the power of LSD came to be understood, however, there was considerable panic. On the basis of Hofmann's light first experience, Sandoz hoped that it might be marketed generally, like barbiturates and tranquilizers. Sandoz thus distributed LSD at cost to many investigators, trying to find a standard use for it.

Sandoz was understandably nervous about some of the wilder aspects of Hofmann's second trip, such as the so-called "out of the body experience," not to mention other aspects which Hofmann has since described as deeply religious. Nevertheless, the people at Sandoz saw a potential for the drug as a "psychotomimetic," or "schizogen." In the literature distributed with LSD, Sandoz recommended it as an agent for producing a model schizophrenia that could be used by psychiatrists and psychologists to explore their patients' states of mind. Sandoz urged that this new substance be tried in only minimal amounts. The earliest studies used miniscule dosages of 20-50 mcgs.

SCATTERING THE SEEDS

THE ENIGMATIC, FLAMBOYANT AL HUBBARD bought 4,000 vials of Sandoz LSD and became an early Johnny Appleseed, repeating a circuit across Canada, down the West Coast to L.A., and back. He gave LSD to many luminaries, including Aldous Huxley and Gerald Heard, and helped establish a long-running LSD clinic in Vancouver, B.C. While most LSD investigators at this time were very cautious, Hubbard saw value in using what were thought to be massive doses, a practice that became common during the 1960s.

Toward the end of the 1950s, Dr. Sidney Cohen, a psychiatrist affiliated with the Veterans Hospital at UCLA, procured large supplies of this novel drug. He became interested when he heard that this substance was a "superior delirient." After self-experimentation, he told his colleagues that although LSD was not a "true delirient," it was worth intensive study. An account of Cohen's first trip can be found in his *The Beyond Within*, which he wrote but attributed to an anonymous doctor.

As Janiger recalls, it was from Cohen's group that social, non-experimental use of LSD might conceivably have arisen in the United States. Janiger said that "these people had first taken it experimentally, because that was the only way it was given at all. Then it was just a short step for people who had taken it to say, 'Let's try it [again]' and to make up some circum-

Hubbard saw value in massive doses.

stance which would justify it. At the beginning, nobody would dare say, 'Let's just take it....' So in somebody's home there would be six or eight people, and they would take the drug. I was at one or two of those, and Huxley would be there, and Heard, and you would meet this strata of people. It was here that you met those people who were a mixture of the investigators, plus those people who were some of their subjects—who had shown a special affinity toward or interest in the drug."

CLINICAL USE

THANKS TO THE SUCCESSES of Freudian and Jungian psychology and to discoveries about mood alteration, researchers in many fields were poised to make a frontal assault on the disordered mind and regarded LSD as very promising.

On the basis of an analogy with malaria and yellow fever, it was thought that duplicating psychosis or schizophrenia using LSD for an eight- or ten-hour period might well produce insights leading to an eventual cure. Little of this work panned out as hoped, since there are significant differences between the LSD state and the various psychoses, in which hallucinations, for instance, are usually auditory rather than visual. The analogy was wrong but it launched a decade of clinical use.

At the start of the 1950s, there were only a handful of papers discussing LSD, but by the end of that decade more than five hundred had appeared. This output is a good measure of how fascinated psychotherapists were with the many possibilities LSD opened up. Much of this work was encouraged and supported by the CIA and later by Army, Air Force, and Navy intelligence. In effect, these agencies triggered an explosion of interest in and use of LSD during the 1960s. In the meantime, more and more research scientists entered this new field, fascinated by its possibilities.

CLINICS OPEN

IN 1953, DR. RONALD SANDISON ESTABLISHED the first LSD clinic open to the public at a small mental hospital in England. Additional centers sprang up in Germany, Italy, France, Holland, Czechoslovakia, several Scandinavian countries, Canada, and the U.S. Nearly all used low dosages in a variety of therapeutic approaches. Slowly they changed the image of this "psychosis-mimicking drug."

Samples of LSD, along with a batch of Sandoz tranquilizers scheduled for study, were sent in 1954 to the Psychiatric Research Institute in Prague, Czechoslovakia. The package was opened by Stanislav Grof when he was a medical student. He was intrigued by the informational leaflet's description of LSD as an agent capable of producing a temporary "model psychosis." Grof tried the LSD in conjunction with a strong flashing light.

Stanislav Grof's First Trip

*We were doing all kinds of experiments. My preceptor, who
gave me LSD, was interested in the EEG among other things,
and also in something that's called "driving the brainwaves"—
which you can do either by using a stroboscopic light or an
acoustic input. And then you study whether the corresponding
brainwaves would pick up the frequencies that you are feeding
into the system.*

*So when I was "peaking" on LSD, a
nurse would come and say, "It's EEG
time." She would take me to this little
cell. I would lie down and she would take
my regular EEG tracing. And then came the time to "drive
my brainwaves." And so she brought the strobe light which we
were using, asked me to close my eyes, put the thing above my
head—and turned it on.*

I experienced being
the universe.

*And this incredible blast of white light came. And the next
thing that I knew was that my consciousness was leaving my
body. Then I lost the clinic. Then I lost Prague. Then I lost
the planet. Then I had a feeling of existing in a totally
disembodied state and literally becoming the universe—
experiencing it. There was "big bang," there were sort of
"white holes," "black holes."*

*While this was happening, the nurse very carefully was
following the instructions—and started at about three cycles,
took it up to sixty and back and forth, and put it carefully in
the middle of the "alpha" range, and then the "theta" range
and "delta" range, and then ended the experiment. And then
I somehow found my body again—and ended up very impressed. So what I did, I joined a group of people who had
access to psychedelic substances.*

14

LSD RESEARCH

ROF WENT ON TO MANAGE LSD RESEARCH on human subjects at the Psychiatric Research Institute in Prague and later did similar work at Spring Grove Mental Hospital near Baltimore. Eventually observing more than 3,500 sessions, he introduced views about the LSD experience quite different from those appearing in the early literature. On the basis of his research, he came to believe that psychiatric concepts were inadequate, and he saw the LSD-induced so-called psychotomimetic reaction as potentially healing—when, for example, a disruptive experience was allowed to continue to resolution.

In Los Angeles, Dr. Nicholas Bercel was active in psychophysiological investigations, publishing articles about LSD in scientific journals and introducing this drug to research and

More than 40,000 mental patients were treated.

medical scientists. In 1954, Janiger, who had been interested in LSD since reading Stoll's first account, was given a chance to try the drug at a mountain retreat. "From that moment on my mind didn't stop for one minute." Janiger wrote Sandoz requesting LSD for a naturalistic study and received a "materials grant"—meaning an ample supply.

Janiger's third subject was an artist who claimed the experience was the equivalent of four years in art school and entreated Janiger to give it to other artists. Janiger wasn't expecting this development, but he eventually gave in and started a subproject in which one hundred artists drew a Kachina doll before, during, and after LSD ingestion. By the end of his investigations in 1962, Janiger had given several thousand administrations of LSD to 875 individuals, many from the creative community in Los Angeles, as well as plumbers, carpenters, and housewives—people from differing educational and ethnic backgrounds.

Until the time research with LSD was dramatically curbed in 1966, more than 40,000 mental patients had received it in dosages running from 20 mcg. to upwards of 2,500 mcg. It was administered privately in some instances, and in others it was given to whole hospital wards. Some people received only one dose; others had as many as 120. In most instances, LSD was used in small amounts as an adjunct to psychotherapy. Other patients took it as a one-time, high-dosage treatment.

Many early investigators screened out psychotics and schizophrenics, but some did not—and often claimed surprising success with such cases. Patients usually received this treatment from only one therapist, but several researchers came to believe that better results could be obtained when the compound was given by several persons.

FEW NEGATIVE RESULTS

THERE WERE SURPRISINGLY FEW NEGATIVE RESULTS. Dr. Sidney Cohen, who was attached professionally to UCLA and the Veterans Hospital in Los Angeles, wrote to sixty-two doctors who had published papers on use of LSD and mescaline/peyote, asking about dangers of such psychedelic treatment. Forty-four replied with detailed comments, covering more than 5,000 patients and volunteers given psychedelics in more than 25,000 sessions. The dosage range in the case of LSD went from 25 mcg. to 1,500 mcg.; 200 mg. to 1,200 mg. was the range for mescaline.

In this survey, not a single physical complication was reported—even when psychedelics were given to alcoholics with generally impaired health. This result was somewhat unexpected, because it had been assumed previously that a diseased liver would produce an adverse reaction. There was also a surprisingly low incidence of major mental disturbances. Despite the profound psychic changes that occur when a person is under the influence of LSD or mescaline, psychotic and other adverse reactions lasting longer than forty-eight hours developed in fewer than 0.2 percent of the cases reported. The attempted suicide rate was just over 0.1 percent. Not one case of addiction was reported, nor any deaths from toxic effects.

If this sampling of 5,000 early psychedelic users is divided into two classes—mentally sound volunteers and people who were mentally unstable—the findings seem even

Risk can be reduced to practically zero.

more encouraging. Among those who volunteered for LSD or mescaline experiments, a major or prolonged psychological complication almost never occurred. In this group, only one instance of a psychotic reaction lasting longer than two days was reported, and there were no suicides. Among the mentally ill, however, prolonged psychotic states were induced in one out of every 550 patients. In this group, one in 830 attempted suicide, and one carried the attempt through.

In evaluating these statistics, it should be pointed out that at the time of this 1960 survey the proper uses of these substances for therapy were not well understood. Some of the negative reactions, furthermore, were deliberately brought about, since many of the doctors were trying to produce model psychoses in their patients. Some even gave the drugs in conjunction with electroshock treatment! Nevertheless, such statistics clearly demonstrate that the dangers in using these powerful drugs are far less than had originally been expected.

METHODS REFINED

NEW AND MORE APPROPRIATE TECHNIQUES have since been introduced, and the methods of administering psychedelics have been refined and have resulted in the reduction of potential hazards. About Cohen's research, Dr. Hanscarl Leuner, an outstanding European expert on psycholytic therapy, says, "Cohen...showed very well how low the relative risk of the therapy is, if it is carried out responsibly by qualified doctors. Thus, we actually are threatened less by adverse results, or severe complications, than we had to assume at the start. Our experience has shown that this risk can be reduced to practically zero in a well-institutionalized therapy, as in our clinic. This holds for the activation of depressions and schizophrenic psychoses, as well as attempted or successful suicides."

Sandoz distributed LSD and psilocybin to licensed researchers all over the world, mostly free of charge. This was done with hopes that a researcher somewhere would find a medical use for these novel compounds. As a result of psychiatric and psychological experiments that ensued, many mental patients and volunteers—examples of the latter are nutritionist Adelle Davis and novelist Ken Kesey—were exposed to the effects of LSD and other psychedelics.

PERSONAL EXPERIMENTATION

THEN THE PICTURE CHANGED. Books like Huxley's first-person accounts, *Exploring Inner Space* by Adelle Davis under the name Jane Dunlap, and additional research such as that with psilocybin by the psychologist Timothy Leary and associates at the Concord, Massachusetts, prison system led to heightened expectations. Millions desired to experience a psychedelic trip in contrast to a psychotomimetic one—which appealed to few.

Lacking access to certified dispensing physicians, many people determined that they would get some one way or another. As psychiatric experimentation expanded into personal experimentation and interest in psychedelics spread, the supply of pure sources manufactured by pharmaceutical houses ran short of the demand.

15

PERSONAL GROWTH

MONG MANY VARIED TECHNIQUES, hypnotism was sometimes used in conjunction with LSD. Other people installed nurses as parent surrogates for their patients. Still others encouraged their patients to act out aggressions during the LSD session, giving them objects to tear up or hit. Some therapists depended primarily upon symbolic interpretation of familiar objects and universal insignia. Others concentrated on dream materials. Some used only LSD, some combined it with Ritalin, Librium, Dramamine, or amphetamine. Others added one or another mind-altering drugs, such as CZ-74, which is a psilocin derivative.

DEALING WITH DIFFICULTIES

GROF PROVIDES A USEFUL START in evaluating the possibility and meaning of a turbulent experience with a psychedelic. He sees the problem as being the definition of a bummer. "Difficult experiences," he declared, "can be the most productive if properly handled and integrated." Grof has emphasized that the best set and setting and quality of LSD cannot guarantee a good trip, if this means easy, pleasant and uncomplicated. "The problem is more management of the experience than the experience itself. We can increase the productiveness of sessions."

Medical benefits have hardly been explored.

SELF-ACTUALIZATION

PSYCHEDELICS FACILITATE PROBLEM-SOLVING AND CREATIVITY, encouraging many who imbibe to take responsibility for their destiny. Canadian researcher Duncan Blewett described the effect of psychedelics on personality as akin to the development of self-awareness, "but which is the beginning of a progression or move from being a self-aware organism to a state of being where an individual responds spontaneously in Zen terms."

Psychedelic drugs encourage the conviction that reality is self-determined rather than predestined. Timothy Leary discussed many aspects of this change in attitude is his books *Neurologic, ExoPsychology*, and *Change Your Brain*. Virtually everyone who has had a psychedelic experience agrees that these substances promote self-actualization and that their use facilitates re-imprinting of more desirable attitudes.

HEALING POWERS

MEDICAL BENEFITS FROM PSYCHEDELICS have hardly been explored. But even the limited preliminary work has given a new understanding of the psychosomatic aspects of ill health. A model for study may be found in the approach taken by the Beneficial Plant Research Association in Carmel, California, which was especially interested in the tonic and other benefits ascribed to the use of coca leaves. This group's "Coca Project" had gone through the red tape to get approval for a comprehensive investigation of coca's efficacy as treatment for painful and spasmodic conditions of the gastrointestinal tract, including gastritis and peptic ulcers; a topical anesthetic in dentistry; a treatment for acute motion sickness; a treatment for laryngitis; a substitute stimulant for coffee in patients who are dependent on coffee but cannot tolerate its irritant effects on the gastrointestinal or urinary systems; a regulator of carbohydrate metabolism in cases of hypoglycemia and diabetes; an adjunctive therapy in programs of weight reduction and physical fitness; and a rapid-acting antidepressant.

As a result of their mental experiences, many "psychonauts" become more aware of their bodys' needs and how to take care of them. These people gave impetus to the renaissance in organic farming, herbal lore, health foods, and many other nature-inspired practices for improving the functioning of the human body.

IMPROVING RELATIONSHIPS

PSYCHEDELICS, WHICH ONCE HELPED CREATE A GENERATION GAP, have also had the effect of improving family relationships, as happened for psychologist Richard Alpert. After taking a large dose of LSD one night, he went to a family reunion the next day. His brother asked, "How's the nut business?" Digging at each other was typical of Alpert's family. It "was our form of love. It was a Jewish, middle-class tradition."

Still affected by his psychedelic state, Alpert saw an arrow coming out of his brother's mouth, slowly crossing the table. In his mind, Alpert reached up, took this arrow and put it next to his spoon. Then he "picked up a heart and blew this over" to his brother and said, "Gee, your kids are getting so incredibly big and handsome."

A look of confusion crossed his brother's face, because Richard wasn't playing the family game. After some silence, his brother sent over another arrow. "Well, you're certainly not growing much hair, are you?" Alpert's response was to reach up for this arrow and set it down on the table. He sent back another heart shape: "Boy, your wife is getting more beautiful all the time."

Alpert says that by mid-afternoon all of the family—husbands and wives and kids gathered in the living room—were experiencing the family bond in a new way, enjoying just being together. "There was this incredible love feast." Nobody wanted to leave. When it was time to break up, everybody stood outside in the street, "and for a long time nobody could get into their car to go. Nobody wanted to break the love bond that had been formed." The gathering, by all reports, "in fact had been a totally unique experience in everybody's life."

His experience and reports of similar effects from many others led Alpert to become interested in the nature of "contact highs," where one person's consciousness in a special way can bring about changes in consciousness of other people. This phenomenon suggests that psychedelic mind expansion is not solely the result of chemical stimulation.

PERSONAL GROWTH

Alpert became interested in "contact highs."

ALMOST FROM THE BEGINNING, psychiatrists and psychologists realized that many effects of this drug had implications relevant to personal growth. R.A. Sandison was one of the earliest practitioners to recognize the potentials of LSD. "There are good reasons for believing that the LSD experience is a manifestation of the psychic unconscious, and that its material can be used in psychotherapy in the same way that dreams, phantasies, and paintings can be used by the psychoanalysts."

IMMEDIATE PERCEPTION

EXPERIMENTATION WITH LARGE, "SINGLE-SHOT" LSD DOSES began in the late 1950s. A great many therapists using this approach started to see in their patients what Sherwood, Stolaroff, and Harman later termed "the stage of immediate perception." They note, "He comes to experience himself in a totally new way and finds that the age-old question 'who am I?' does have a significant answer. He experiences himself as a far greater being than he had ever imagined, with his conscious self a far smaller fraction of the whole than he had realized. Furthermore, he sees that his own self is by no means so separate from other selves and the universe about him as he might have thought. Nor is the existence of this newly experienced self so intimately related to his corporeal existence. These realizations, while not new to mankind, and possibly not new to the subject in the intellectual sense, are very new in an experiential sense. That is, they are new in the sense that makes for altered behavior. The individual sees clearly that some of his actions are not in line with his new knowledge and that changes are obviously called for."

16

ACID THERAPY

B Y THE TIME of the Josiah Macy, Jr. Foundation conference on LSD at the end of the 1950s, it had become clear that this semi-synthetic drug seemed to affirm the concepts of most of the psychological schools. The Freudians were using LSD to abreact their patients and to explore Oedipal and other notions. The Jungians found that this drug manifested mandalas and rebirth experiences in their patients.

A fascinating account of an extended Freudian treatment appears in My Self and I, written by the Kirlian researcher and parapsychologist Thelma Moss, under the name Constance Newland. Dr. Donald Blair, an English consulting psychiatrist, summed up his view of LSD's results: "People who have had psychotherapy or psychoanalysis for some time, as much as eight years, and haven't gotten anywhere, do so with the drug; it does break resistance....You get neurotic patients who have been to numerous therapists, analysts, and they don't get better. Then they come to one of us who are using LSD and thanks to the effect of the drug, they do get better."

TRANSFERENCE

A CHARACTERISTIC OF THE LSD EXPERIENCE particularly fascinating to Freudian analysts has been its power to cause the patient to regress to early traumas, which could then be relieved. This chemical is still used as an aid in

"transference." Dr. Gordon Johnsen, of
Modum Bads Nervesantoriun in Norway,
elaborates: "If we get sexual perverts, for
example, we may question what kind of
treatment to give them; we want to find

Patients could regress to early traumas.

out a little more about them. We could use three or four
weeks finding out, but we shorten that and say we will
try if we can find out more with one or two LSD
sessions. We use small doses then. We find that the
symptoms are clearer; they are willing to speak more
openly to us; we can get a clearer picture of the diagnosis. We have used it in that way to save time."

ALCOHOLISM

RECORDS KEPT OF ALCOHOLIC RECOVERY RATES following
ingestion of LSD constitute the firmest quantitative data
so far on the effects of this substance. They are especially
impressive when one considers that independent studies
using different methods achieved substantially identical
results. In most instances, the patients were chosen from
the worst cases that could be found. Some studies using
different procedures have not been as successful.

Abram Hoffer treated more than 800 hardcore alcoholics in the Canadian LSD program. He reported that
"When psychedelic therapy is given to alcoholics using
methods described in the literature, about one-third will
remain sober after the therapy is completed and one-third
will be benefitted. If schizophrenics and malvarians [those
showing a particularly purplish component of urine] are
excluded from LSD therapy, the results should be better
by about 30 percent. There are no published papers using
psychedelic therapy which show it does not help about 50
percent of the treated group...."

"Our conclusion after 13
years of research is that properly
used, LSD therapy can convert a
large number of alcoholics into

LSD therapy can convert many alcoholics into sober members of society.

sober members of society.... Even more important is the fact that this can be done very quickly, and therefore very economically. Whereas with standard therapy one bed might be used to treat about 4 to 6 patients per year, with LSD one can easily treat up to 36 patients per bed per year."

SUPERIOR TREATMENT

THE MAJORITY OF LSD THERAPISTS AGREED just before being denied access to LSD that this drug is superior to other forms of treatment in its effect on the whole range of neuroses and disorders that ordinarily respond to psychoanalysis. Typical reports indicate that even with severe problems, only 10 to 15 percent of patients failed to achieve any improvement. When Hollywood Hospital in Vancouver, B.C., followed up eighty-nine patients for an average of fifty-five months, it found that 55 percent had a total remission of their problem, 34 percent were improved, and 11 percent were unchanged.

At the University of Göttingen's Psychiatric Hospital, Dr. Hanscarl Leuner's results, independently rated, showed 76 percent of the patients with character neuroses, depressive reactions, anxiety, phobias, or conversion-hysteria were "greatly improved" or "recovered." In an evaluation of his work at Marborough Day Hospital in London, Dr. Ling states that "an analysis of 43 patients treated privately...shows that 34 are completely well and socially well-adjusted. Six are improved, one abandoned treatment, one had to leave for Africa before treatment was finished, and one failed to respond satisfactorily, so treatment was abandoned."

Best results were with motivated neurotics.

Most of the successful reports on the treatment of mental patients with LSD deal with neurotic patients who have been motivated to get well. There seems to be tacit agreement among therapists that LSD is not effective dealing with psychoses. Practitioners who have undertaken LSD treatment of schizophrenics have been regarded as brave or reckless.

NOT FOR EVERYONE

LSD DOES NOT WORK VERY WELL with patients whose mental derangements are seriously advanced. It may precipitate a worsening of the condition. Nevertheless, a large body of evidence indicates that those who have administered LSD in such cases have often obtained positive reactions that are worthy of broader consideration.

Dr. Fred F. Langner used LSD effectively with a number of severely disturbed persons, mainly schizophrenics. After he used LSD in over 2,000 patient sessions, he concluded that pseudo-neurotics and paranoid schizophrenics do not respond favorably and may, in fact, suffer clinical setbacks. However, he observed that schizoid personalities, whose egos are not too brittle, may through LSD have their first experience with "feeling." One of his patients said, "I know now that I never knew what people were talking about when they talked about feelings until I took LSD. I didn't know until toward the end of my second year in therapy that feelings could be good as well as bad."

As mentioned earlier, Huxley described LSD as a means of insight into the "Other World." As an instrument of therapy, it has brought many back into contact with reality. Here is another paradox, another example of the unifying action of LSD.

Paranoid schizophrenics do not respond favorably.

Consider a comment by Norma McDonald, a recovered schizophrenic: "One of the most encouraging things which has happened to me in recent years was the discovery that I could talk to normal people who had had the experience of taking mescaline or lysergic acid, and they would accept the things I told them about my adventures in mind without asking stupid questions or withdrawing into a safe, smug world of disbelief. Schizophrenia is a lonely illness and friends are of great importance. I have needed true friends to help me to believe in myself when I doubted my own mind, to encourage me with their praise, jolt me out of unrealistic ideas with their honesty, and teach me by their example how to work and play. The discovery of LSD-25 by those who work in the field of psychiatry has widened my circle of friends."

ACCOUNTS

THE BEST ACCOUNTS OF ACID THERAPY in English are Grof's *LSD Pyschotherapy* and Hausner and Segal's *The Highway to Mental Health: LSD Psychotherapy*. The latter details Hausner's use of LSD as an adjunct to psychotherapy for more than twenty years in Czechoslovakia. In reviewing this volume, John C. Rhead, who participated in LSD experiments as a doctor at Spring Grove Hospital, wholeheartedly welcomed it "as an encouraging sign that good work with psychedelics is still going on somewhere in the world."

Pointing to its "constant theme...of corrective/healing experience emerging from the patient's own subconscious," Rhead says "the fundamental belief in the capacity of the human psyche to be self-healing under the proper circumstances is but one of the many striking parallels between Dr. Hausner's conclusions and those of the group at the Maryland Psychiatric Research Center.... Many passages of Dr. Hausner's book sound very much like the things that my colleagues/friends in Maryland and I have thought, said and/or written...."

Good work with psychedelics is still going on some- where in the world.

Rhead adds "that examples of these similarities are found in the following areas: the critical importance of interpersonal trust in conducting successful psychotherapy with psychedelics, the use of music, the importance of having the therapist/guide experience LSD as part of an ethically adequate training to do this type of work, the unique value of artistic productions by the patient for both assessment of functioning as well as integration of emerging subconscious material, the presentation during the LSD session of significant objects from the patient's life, e.g., photographs, in order to stimulate associations and fresh insights and perspectives, the need to include the concepts of many diverse schools of psychotherapeutic thought in order to understand and utilize LSD, the importance of working through and integrating the experiences that emerge during LSD sessions and the fundamental value or reality of the mystic or peak experiences that frequently occur...."

Rhead believes "that these similarities are the result of two groups of relatively blind but curious and well-intentioned investigators independently having taken the time to grope rather thoroughly over the entire elephant. As is commonly noted in the literature of comparative religion, there really does appear to be only one elephant."

LSD VILIFIED

ONCE LEGAL RESTRICTIONS WERE ENACTED, promising scientific studies were curtailed. Then head of the Food and Drug Administration James Goddard declared that alleged creative and other benefits from psychedelics were *"pure bunk."* Janiger, reflecting on the stigma suddenly thrust on LSD researchers, said that he had come to be perceived as "a villain who was, you know, trying to seduce people into taking it. It was absolutely bizarre! From the heroes, we were suddenly some creatures who were seducing people into changing their consciousness."

TRIPS INTERRUPTED

SUCH WIDESPREAD USE OF PSYCHEDELICS released enormous creative impulses that continue to affect us all. Whether or not one uses these substances, their effects have permeated society down to the grass roots. Many hoped that these powerful compounds could be absorbed in society in legitimate ways. Ivan Tors, producer of the *Flipper* TV series, gave up LSD when laws banning psychedelics went into effect. "My upbringing was such that the thought of doing something illegal would put me in a negative state, and thus interfere with my LSD experiences. I feel this is true of others as well, and may account for many of the untoward reactions of those who use LSD in the underground."

REGULATIONS

EVEN THOUGH SEVERAL DECADES have passed since the psychedelic panic of the mid-1960s, federal regulations and hospital "Human Rights" committees continue to block requests to use psychedelics on humans. They are afraid of negative publicity and lawsuits. When Walter Houston Clark inserted a questionnaire addressed to research professionals in *Behavior Today,* and the *Newsletter* of the Association for Humanistic Psychology, nearly all who replied stated that they would like to do psychedelic research.

Of the first hundred people who responded to Clark's request, half had been associated at one time with con-trolled drug studies. Asked why they weren't engaged in such work any more, eighty-one mentioned governmental red tape, sixty cited other bureaucratic obstruction, seventy-eight wrote that they weren't able to secure clear-ance, and fifty-three indicated lack of funding as "large reasons." Asked to rate the promise of psychedelics in the mental health area, "assuming opportunity for controlled experimentation," none called it negative, one thought it might be neutral, seven perceived it as meager, fifteen felt it was moderate, thirty-four considered it high, and thirty-six believed that investigation of psychedelics held out "breakthrough" possibilities. Another seven didn't answer this question. "Do I feel any patients are being denied an experience of significant value as a result of non-acceptance of LSD as a therapeutic tool?" Dr. Langner asked. "Yes, I do."

LSD IN NATURE

WITH THE CLOSING OF THE DECADE of clinical use came perhaps the most important discovery since Dr. Hofmann first synthesized LSD. Late in the summer of 1959, Hofmann received a parcel of seeds from a researcher he had made contact with while investigating the sacred Mexican fungi. The seeds were of what was then called *Rivea corymbosa*, otherwise known as *ololiuqui*, a Mexican morning glory. In the summer of 1960,

Turbina corymbosa

Richard Evans Schultes

Hofmann isolated the active principles and identified them chemically. They were ergot alkaloids. "From the phytochemical point of view," commented Hofmann when disclosing these results, "this finding was unexpected and of particular interest, because lysergic acid alkaloids, which had hitherto been found only in lower fungi in the genus *Claviceps*, were now, for the first time, indicated for the higher plants, in the phanerogamic family Convolvulaceae." First synthesized in a laboratory, LSD was now found to have a counterpart in nature.

17

CREATIVITY

 LARGE NUMBER of testimonials indicates that LSD can dissolve creative blockage. Many examples are presented in Masters and Houston's *Psychedelic Art* and in Metzner's *The Ecstatic Adventure*, which contains reports from participants in the Menlo Park creativity studies, including two architects and an

LSD can dissolve creative blocks.

engineer-physicist who was working on a model for a photon. A general presentation of that creativity research can be found in Charles Tart's *Altered States of Consciousness.* Stanley Krippner also summarized the findings of nine major studies in this area.

ARCHITECTURE

A NOTABLE EARLY EXAMPLE was architect Kyoshi Izumi's design of a psychiatric hospital in Canada. He was given LSD by Humphry Osmond before he made several visits to traditionally designed mental institutions in order to evaluate the effects of their design upon people in altered states of consciousness.

Izumi found that tiles on walls glistened eerily and recessed closets yawned like huge, dark caverns. He noticed that raised hospital beds were too high for patients to sit on and still touch the floor with their feet and a sense of time was lost because of the lack of clocks and calendars. Worst of all were the long corridors.

Osmond called the thousands of square feet of polished tiles in these institutions "illusion-producing machines par excellence, and very expensive ones at that. If your perception is a little unstable, you may see your dear old father peering out at you from the walls...."

These insights, which were made clear through his use of LSD, resulted in Izumi's design for the ideal mental hospital, which was commended for outstanding architectural advancement by the Joint Information Service of the American Psychiatric Association. The first hospital constructed based on his plans was built in Yorkton, Saskatchewan, and was imitated soon after in Haverford, Pennsylvania. The prototype has been reproduced several times since, mainly in Canada.

Bonnie Golightly and I summarized distinguishing features. The Yorkton hospital consists of small, cottage-like clusters of rooms, thirty to a unit, joined together by underground passageways. There are many windows, low and unbarred, eliminating the old, dismal barnlike aspect of mental hospitals. The walls are painted in pleasant, flat colors, and each patient has his own room in one or another of the clusters, rather than a bed in an austere, nearly bare ward. The beds are low to the floor, and the rooms

It met patient needs without sacrificing utility.

are furnished with regard to making it easier to define the floor as a mere floor, not a pit. Also, the furniture is comfortable and not unlike that with which the patient is familiar at home. The closet problem has been solved by installing large, movable cabinets which the patient can clearly see possess both a back and a front. Clocks and calendars abound, while floor tiles are sparingly used. The emphasis throughout puts patient needs foremost, without sacrificing utility.

GRAPHIC ART

IN 1955, BERLIN, GUTHRIE, WELDER, Goodell, and Wolff reported on four prominent graphic artists who made paintings during an LSD experience. A panel of art critics judged the paintings as having greater value than the artists' usual work—noting that use of color was more vivid and lines were bolder, though the technical execution was somewhat poorer. Similar results were reported by Frank Barron in *Creativity and Psychological Health*, and by Janiger, who it has been already mentioned, wrote in *The California Clinician* about his experiments with LSD and artists drawing Indian Kachina dolls.

CONTRASTING RESULTS

BY WAY OF CONTRAST, studies made with volunteers who were not particularly interested in LSD's creative potential reflected no significant changes in creativity. William McGlothlin, Sidney Cohen, and others, and then the team of Zegans, Pollard, and Brown, reported these findings in the *Journal of Nervous and Mental Diseases* and in the *Archives of General Psychiatry*. Six months after three 200-mcg. LSD sessions, the McGlothlin team found only one major distinction. Sixty-two percent of their subjects reported "a greater appreciation of music." An increase in the number of records bought, time spent in museums, and number of musical events attended was also significantly greater than for two control groups, who were given either 25 mcg. of LSD or 20 mg. of amphetamine per session.

Cohen wrote: "All that can be said at this time about the effect of LSD on the creative process is that a strong subjective feeling of creativeness accompanies many of the experiences." The Zegans group concluded that "the administration of LSD-25 to a relatively unselected group of people, for the purpose of enhancing their creative ability, is not likely to be successful."

On the other hand, the Institute for Psychedelic Research at San Francisco State College, headed by Fadiman, Harman, McKim, Mogar, and Stolaroff, came to remarkably positive findings when they gave LSD and mescaline to professionals who were faced with technical problems that they had been unable to solve. Hypothesizing that "through carefully structured regimen, a learning experience with lingering creative increases could result," this group administered psychedelics to twenty-two volunteers. By the time of their report in November 1965, six had already seen concrete benefits in their work. At that point, the Institute's access to psychedelics was terminated. Comments made by some of the people taking part in this project indicate something of the way LSD affected their thinking:

Fear of mistakes diminishes.

Creativity & LSD

Looking at the same problem with [psychedelic] materials, I was able to consider it in a much more basic way, because I could form and keep in mind a much broader picture.

I had great visual [mental] perceptibility; I could imagine what was wanted, needed, or not possible with almost no effort.

Ideas came up with a speed that was breathtaking.

I dismissed the original idea entirely, and started to approach the graphic problem in a radically different way. That was when things began to happen. All kinds of different possibilities came to mind.

Diminished fear of making mistakes or being embarrassed.

I was impressed with the intensity of concentration, the forcefulness and exuberance with which I could proceed toward the problem.

In what seemed like 10 minutes, I had completed the problem, having what I considered—and still consider—a classic solution.

Brought about almost total recall of a course that I had had in thermodynamics, something that I had never given any thought about in years.

ARTISTS' REACTION

KRIPPNER SURVEYED 180 PROFESSIONAL ARTISTS reported to
have had at least one psychedelic experience. Eighteen, as
it turned out, had never taken a psychoactive chemical.
These artists, it might be noted, included "two award-
winning film-makers, a Guggenheim Fellow in poetry, a
recipient of Ford, Fulbright, and Rockefeller study grants
in painting, several college faculty members, and numerous
musicians, actors, and writers," mainly from the New York
area but with a significant proportion from around the
world.

When asked how psychedelic experiences influenced
their art, none said his or her work had suffered, although some admitted that their friends might disagree
with this judgment. Five stated that their psychedelic
experiences had not influenced their work one way or the
other, but most were enthusiastic about the effects. The
painter Arlene Sklar-Weinstein, who had gone through
only one LSD experience, is representative: "It opened
thousands of doors for me and dramatically changed the content,
intent, and style of my work."

Most experienced a change in their creative approach.

Of the 180 artists surveyed, 114
said that their psychedelic experi-
ences had affected the content of their work; they mainly
cited their use of eidetic, or closed-eyes, imagery as a
source of subject matter. Fully 131 responded that there
had been a noticeable improvement in their artistic
technique, most often mentioning a greater ability to use
colors. In addition, 142 attributed a change in creative
approach to the psychedelics. Many indicated that dormant interests in art and music had been activated by
psychedelic sessions.

WRITER'S BLOCK

LSD HAS HELPED TO END WRITER'S BLOCK. Ling and
Buckman's *The Use of LSD and Ritalin in the Treatment of*

Neurosis cites the example of a well-known European writer whose major work, translated into twelve languages, was written subsequent to LSD usage. Previously, he had had a "burning desire" to write but had been unable to finish a single manuscript.

Under the influence of LSD, he was confronted with a sudden awareness that he could die. "With this horror of death realized, I started to experience a most fantastic happiness with the realization that after all I do not have to die now." It freed him as an artist; he no longer felt he was writing "with my neck under the guillotine." He wrote, "I am no longer afraid of putting one letter after the other to say what I want and this is linked with an enormous number of things, such as speechlessness and inarticulateness. The feeling of being dumb, not being able to express myself, was probably one of my most unpleasant inner feelings....I [now] seem capable of expressing what many people would love to express but for which they cannot find the words. I did not find the words before because I tried to avoid saying the essential things."

Krippner quotes the Dutch writer Ronny van den Eerenbeemt as having responded similarly: "Van den Eerenbeemt said, 'When I was very young, I started writing stories and poems. The older I got, the more I had a feeling of not being able to find something really worthwhile to write about. My psychedelic experiences taught me that what I used to do was no more than scratch the surface of life. After having seen and felt the center of life, through the psychedelics, I now think I do have something worthwhile to write about.'"

At the conclusion of his survey of the effects from LSD and similar psychedelics, Krippner summarized that "Little scientific research has been undertaken with psychedelic drugs since advances in information theory, brain physiology, and the study of consciousness...have revolutionized our understanding of those areas. This increase in knowledge and theoretical sophistication affords science a unique opportunity to study the creative act. Creativity has been a perpetual enigma; now, at last, it may be prepared to divulge its secrets."

MOTIVATION

A FINAL POINT ABOUT THE CREATIVE PROCESS. It does not seem to have too much to do with conventional I.Q., as measured by existing tests. Frank Barron, while a research psychologist at the University of California Institute of Personality Assessment, compared more than 5,000 productive and creative individuals with others in their field who had similar I.Q. but limited productivity.

Cosmological Commitment

The thing that was important was something that might be called a cosmological commitment. It was a powerful motive to create meaning and to leave a testament of the meaning which that individual found in the world, and in himself in relation to the world. This motive emerged in many ways, but we came across it over and over again when we compared highly creative individuals with those of equal intellectual ability as measured by I.Q. tests, but of less actual creative ability. The intense motivation having to do with this making of meaning—or finding meaning and communicating it in one form or another—was the most important difference between our criterion and control groups....

I think that as a result of the psychedelic experience there's a heightened sense of the drama of life, including its brevity, and a realization both of the importance of one's individual life and of the fact that a sacred task has been given to the individual in the development of the self.

18

BEYOND LSD

I N THE FUTURE, psychedelic explorers will have an opportunity to experiment with an array of compounds that
can provide wide variations on the basic LSD experience. Alexander Shulgin has noted the implications of
synthesizing drug analogs of known psychedelics. He said
that "The time will come when we'll separate all our senses
and capabilities—the visual from the auditory, the tactile
from the sense of smell as well as wit, intellectual capability,
creativity—and be able to enhance them with drugs."

Being able to choose psychoactive compounds with more
specific effects than LSD, mescaline, and psilocybin has
already resulted in more subtle possibilities, along with giant
strides in our understanding of how alterations in psychoactive molecular structures affect their duration, as well as
empathetic, visual, and other qualities. New psychedelic
substances may have some surprising effects. In the future,
we may have psychedelics that go beyond LSD for power
and interest.

SYNERGY

RELATED TO THESE DEVELOPMENTS have been interest and
experimentation in the synergistic effects derived from
ingesting different psychedelics within a relatively close
timespan. Use of MDMA to induce a relaxed mental set
prior to taking LSD, or employment of DMT together with
another psychedelic, qualitatively alter the consequences that

would ordinarily come about from taking just a single compound. Synergism—the simultaneous action of separate agencies which, together, have greater total effect than the sum of their individual effects—is a well recognized quality of drugs and seems especially characteristic of psychedelics.

L.M. Boyd, who has written a syndicated newspaper column about oddities called "Grab Bag," once gave an analogy in terms of food. He said, "You don't get out of beans what you get out of meat. You don't get out of rice what you get out of meat. But although the vegetable proteins are incomplete separately, they're complementary. So you do get out of beans and rice together what you get out of meat." Curious.

EASTERN INFLUENCE

CONCEPTS AND TRADITIONS FROM EASTERN RELIGIONS and shamanic procedures will continue to be assimilated into Western culture and they will alter our sense of human potentialities. Grof has illustrated this point by describing how he tried to fit his observations from LSD experiences into the Freudian outlook about psychological functioning for several years. Eventually, he had to give this up, since this hardly took into account "ancestral, racial, evolutionary, past incarnation, precognition and telepathy, planetary and extra-planetary, and time and space travel" phenomena, as Michael Horowitz summed up Grof's findings, that regularly crop up in such sessions.

Huxley described his expectation about the major influence from psychedelics as essentially producing "an everyday mysticism underlying and giving significance to everyday rationality, everyday tasks and duties, everyday human relationships."

They become everyday mystics. That, no doubt, is occurring now and will in the future. This is but one of the prominent areas catalyzed by these drugs, however, and their eventual impact upon society involves much more.

CONTRIBUTIONS

THAT EXPERIENCES CAUSED BY PSYCHEDELICS have now become much more manageable is evidenced by the closing of psyche-delic rescue services and a decline in trippers seeking help at hospitals. We can anticipate that future usage will make signifi-cant contributions to psychological and physical health, to creative innovation, and to an understanding of some of the stranger aspects of human behavior.

Science fiction writer Norman Spinrad emphasizes that psychochemistry has created states of consciousness "that had never existed before." Taking a psychedelic dramatically changes the traditional notions of free will. Spinrad's view is that psycho-chemicals are a declaration of independence from the minds we were born with, and that hence "we will no longer be able to count on our 'naturally evolved' brain chemistry as a benchmark of sanity."

Even though many psychedelic experiences do not have much resonance, others have consequences all out of proportion, especially when people apply the heightened sensitivity prompted by these substances to disciplines that they have pursued for years.

Shulgin provides a good example when he described in a book entitled *Mind Drugs* how he has been able, under the influence of MDA-like compounds, to twist molecular arrange-ments around in his head, and thus could view them differently and from unusual angles. That ability has turned out to be unusually productive. A more disquieting example, to

> *The psychedelic experience changes our notions of free will.*

emphasize the amorality of science, is that of a futurist associ-ated with a think tank on the East Coast who spent much time during his first psychedelic session considering bombing patterns over China.

As these examples suggest, the consequences from the experiences of psychedelic trips might come to have great significance. It should be emphasized that even if all psychedelic substances were to be wiped off the face of the earth, the tremendous effects they have already catalyzed would nonetheless continue on by themselves. This aspect of psychedelic consequences was perhaps most clearly stated when a physician remarked to a medical gathering that although he hadn't actually ever taken a psychedelic, LSD had "changed my life completely."

The future impact of psychedelics will be the sum of changes produced in millions of individual sessions. Most will be considered beneficial by their users, a very small number will not. May it be, as Alan Watts hoped, that we will have accepted the opportunities offered and be "swimming in the ocean of relativity as joyously as dolphins in the water."

Physical Health

IN SOME CASES, THERE ARE LONG-LASTING PHYSICAL EFFECTS from tripping. Many doctors have reported, often with pleased surprise, that their patients have achieved spontaneous relief from organic ailments after using LSD. Dr. T.T.

Many get relief from organic aliments.

Peck, Jr., for instance, at the Josiah Macy, Jr. Conference on LSD, remarked that "in treating patients for various and sundry psychological complaints, we found that some would come back a week or two later and say, 'The headache is gone.' We asked, 'What headache?' They replied, 'Oh, the headache I've had for 10 or 15 years.'"

A substantial number of cases entered in medical records have now established LSD as a competent agent in the cure of such physical ailments as arthritis, partial paralysis, migraine headaches, hysterical deafness, skin rashes, and so on.

Peck reported on his study of 216 mentally disturbed patients who were given LSD. Forty-six of these patients suffered also from some physical illness—including various forms of arthritis, asthmas that did not respond to hypnosis, migraine headaches, and lasting rashes. Thirty-one of the forty-six made an "excellent" recovery from their symptoms, while five others found marked relief. Other doctors who have treated similar problems with LSD have found that such stubborn conditions can often be eradicated in the course of a few sessions.

In their book on the use of LSD in the treatment of neurosis, Drs. Ling and Buckman list five case histories of successful migraine cures—all of which had previously been considered hopeless. They also give a full-length account of LSD's use in treating a severe case of supposedly hopeless psoriasis, with impressive photographs showing the patient before and after treatment. S. Kuromaru and co-workers in Japan have shown that this multi-functional substance can be used with good results even in the treatment of phantom limb pain.

PAIN REDUCTION

THE MOST ENRAPTURED ACID HEADS are well aware that LSD is not—and never can be—a panacea, a solution to all of this planet's problems. This most powerful psychoactive compound hasn't been demonstrated to keep us from aging or to reverse the course of fatal diseases. However, it does, without a doubt, offer important benefits for people confronted with terminal illness. This is an area in which research, particularly at the Veterans Hospital in Los Angeles, the Menninger Clinic in Topeka, and Spring Grove Hospital near Baltimore, has impressed skeptics.

DYING WITH LSD

HUXLEY DESERVES SPECIAL CREDIT as the inspiration for this research, because he wrote about its possibilities in his last novel, *Island.* He took LSD on his deathbed. The medical world became aware of LSD's ability to change the perceptions of death in the mid-1960s when the American Medical Association published a report on fifty dying patients who had been given the drug in a Chicago hospital. In this preliminary study conducted by noted psychiatrist Dr. Eric Kast, LSD was shown to be more effective as an analgesic or pain reliever than any of the frequently used morphine derivatives: "In...50 patients, most with advanced cancer and some with gangrene, LSD relieved pain for considerably longer periods than such powerful drugs as meperidine and dihydro-morphinone.... On the average, freedom from pain lasted two hours with 100 mg. meperidine, three hours with 2 mg. dihydro morphinone and 92 hours with 100 mcg. LSD."

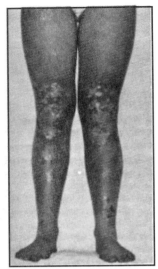 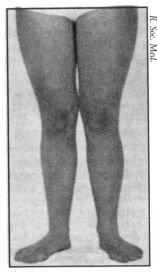

Before and after treatment of severe psoriasis
with LSD (right) and Ritalin (left).

To the amazement of observers, terminal patients
given LSD changed in their attitudes—from depression,
apathy, and anguish to sensitivity, poignancy, and deep
feeling for people. They movingly expressed gratitude for
life itself. LSD seemed to enable many to face death with
equanimity.

Instead of denial or fright, these patients generally
experienced a feeling of being at one with the universe
and looked upon dying as merely another event in eternal
existence. "It was a common experience," wrote Kast, "for
the patient to remark casually on his deadly disease and
then comment on the beauty of a certain sensory impression." Such desirable emotional balance lasted long after
LSD's pain-killing action wore off, for up to two weeks in
some cases. Later studies have confirmed how impressive
the short but profound impact of LSD can be for the
dying.

19

PLANT SOURCES

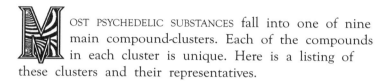OST PSYCHEDELIC SUBSTANCES fall into one of nine main compound-clusters. Each of the compounds in each cluster is unique. Here is a listing of these clusters and their representatives.

MORNING GLORIES

WHEN THE CONQUISTADORES SUBDUED THE AZTECS, early chroniclers recorded that the Indians made religious and medicinal use of peyote, another psychoactive plant named *tlitliltzin,* and a small lentil-like seed called *ololiuqui.* The third, alleged to have been used also for purposes of divination, came from a vine known in the Náhuatl language as *coaxihuitl,* or "snakeplant."

When he published some botanical notes by the Spanish physician Hernández, Ximénez stated in 1615 in regard to *ololiuqui:* "It matters little that this plant be here described or that Spaniards be made acquainted with it." He expressed the generally negative Spanish attitude.

Hernandez and others had described the plant, indicating that it was held in great veneration, and illustrations—as in the *Florentine Codex*—suggested that it was a member of the familiar bindweed or Morning Glory family (*Convolvulaceae*), but knowledge of this species and its seed was lost to all but a few Zapotec, Chinantec, Mazatec, and Mixtec tribes—dwelling mostly in Oaxaca in southern Mexico—for more than four centuries.

DIVINATION

THE ETHNOBOTANIST SCHULTES sent samples of a cultivated Mexican Morning Glory to Hofmann in 1959, when it was still called *Rivea corymbosa*. He had seen it employed in divination by a Zapotec shaman in Oaxaca.

Corymbosa is now considered one of five *Turbina* species—the only one appearing in the Americas. Though there are more than 500 species of *Convolvulaceae* widely scattered around the globe, they seem to have been used for their psychoactive properties only by tribes in the New World.

Kathlene Harrison

Psychedelic Morning Glory
(*Ipomoea violacea*).

Psychedelic Clusters

Cluster 1: The LSD Family, the major catalyst opening the psychedelic age and the archetype

Cluster 2: Peyote, Mescaline and San Pedro, a cluster once considered the most powerful; the door opener for psychedelics in the 1950s

Cluster 3: Marijuana and Hashish, the earliest recorded psychedelics, which exhibit synergistic action with all of the others

Cluster 4: Psilocybian Mushrooms, the easily identified, gently persuasive and yet powerfully mind-changing fungi containing psilocybin and/or psilocin that re-introduced an appreciation of psychedelic effects in the late 1970s

Cluster 5: Nutmeg and MDA, the empathic compounds that create few visuals, stimulating research into discrete psychedelic effects

Cluster 6: DMT, DET, DPT and Other Short-Acting Tryptamines, a family of varying intensities but including the psychedelic that's the most impressive visually

Cluster 7: Ayahuasca, Yage and Harmaline, the "visionary vine" complex from the Amazon that is a telepathic healer

Cluster 8: Iboga and Ibogaine, the bush from Africa used in initiatory rites and by hunters to produce extended stillness, and its principal alkaloid that produces vivid imagery and stimulation

Cluster 9: Fly Agaric, Panther Caps and Soma, the colorful, fascinating, sometimes frightful, legendary mushrooms that have been used shamanically and may have, in Wasson's words, provoked "the religious idea in homo sapiens."

SACRAMENTS

DON THOMAS MACDOUGALL reported that seeds of *Ipomoea violacea* were used as sacraments by certain Zapotecs, sometimes in conjunction with *ololiuqui* and sometimes not. These Morning Glory seeds, called *badoh negro,* come from the same botanical family, but are jet black rather than brown and are long and angular rather than round. When analyzed, the *badoh negro* seeds were found to have the same mentally-affecting amides as *Turbina (Rivea) corymbosa,* except that ergometrine—a strong uterotonic—showed up in place of lysergol.

Some people believe that *badoh negro* is the seed the early Spanish records referred to as *tlitliltzin*—the Náhuatl word for "black," slightly altered by a reverential suffix. These seeds turned out to be stronger in psychoactivity than *ololiuqui.* The total

alkaloid content of the *Rivea (Turbina)* is 0.012 percent, while that of *Ipomoea* is about 0.06 percent. American varieties of *Ipomoea violacea* containing *d*-lysergic acid amides are: Heavenly Blue, Pearly Gates, Flying Saucers, Blue Star, Summer Skies, and Wedding Bells.

A CHANGE IN A MOLECULE

IF YOU COMPARE LSD-25 and the main ingredient of *ololiuqui*, you'll see that the only difference is substitution of two hydrogen atoms in the amide group for two ethyl radicals. This slight change in the molecule makes LSD 50 to 100 times more active than the central ingredient in Morning Glories. *The First Book of Sacraments* of the Church of the Tree of Life compares the experiential differences between the seeds and LSD:

The First Book of Sacraments

The effect of these alkaloids in combination is similar to LSD and other hallucinogens, but more tranquil. Some people experience nausea during the first hour. Large doses are not recommended. After the major effects have worn off one usually feels very soft and relaxed....

It is not advisable for people with a history of hepatitis, jaundice, or other serious liver disease to take [these] lysergic acid amides. Because several of the alkaloids in this family of sacraments have powerful uterus-stimulating properties we recommend that they not be taken by pregnant women.

HAWAIIAN WOODROSES

CHEMICAL INVESTIGATIONS HAVE CONFIRMED the appearance of ergot alkaloids in other *Convolvulaceae*–bindweed or Morning Glory—species, notably in the *Argyreia* genus, in at least eleven species, and the large Hawaiian woodrose and in *Stictocardia tilafolia,* which contains six amides of lysergic acid in its seed.

NOT A ROSE

OF THESE PLANTS, THE ONE THAT HAS BEEN MOST USED as a psychedelic is the baby Hawaiian Woodrose. This actually isn't a rose, but rather a woody climbing vine or liana with silvery foliage and violet flowers. When dried, the leaves turn tan on the outside and a light, warm saddle brown on the inside. The pod has the color of caramel. This beautiful arrangement has resulted in its use in floral displays and corsages. Native to India, it is now cultivated throughout the world's tropical regions.

Otto Degener in his monumental *Flora Hawaiiensis* in the 1930s described the baby Hawaiian Woodrose as thriving in the Islands in drier regions at lower elevations, flowering during August and early September, and then becoming "a prolific seeder, the ground under a large vine often being crowded with erect, bud-covered seedlings." According to William Emboden, this has been used as an inebriant by poorer Hawaiians. It has been only occasionally taken by those in the American drug subculture, though advertised in *High Times*. At art fairs in California, a mixture of five of these baby seeds ground up together with ginseng, damiana, gotu kola, and bee pollen and pressed into a date has been sold under the name "Utopian Bliss Balls."

POTENCY

LYSERGIC ACID AMIDES ARE QUITE CONCENTRATED in the seeds of this ornamental, much more so than in psychedelic Morning Glories. Four to six seeds, the contents of one or two pods, are the equivalent of 100 to 150 *Ipomoea* Morning Glory seeds and will produce a full-blown experience. The result is generally more tranquil than what is induced by LSD.

While LSD is perceived by most users as having stimulant effects, to which a few people are particularly sensitive, the botanical sources have more of a slowing or depressant effect. Some users complain that they have had a hangover, which has been characterized by Emboden as possibly involving "nausea, constipation, vertigo, blurred vision, and physical inertia." More often, however, these seeds have invigorated their users, leaving them feeling as though they had been on vacation afterwards.

Lysergic acid amides including chanoclavine, ergine, isoergine, and ergonovine are present in the psychoactive *Argyreia* species—*speciosa, acuta, bernesii, capitata, osyrensis, wallichii, splendens, hainanensis, obtusifolia* and *pseudorubicunda*—mainly concentrated in the seeds. The larger Hawaiian woodrose, or *Merremia tuberosa*, also produces such amides, but like the others is not nearly as potent as the baby Hawaiian woodrose. A thesis published by a Harvard graduate student illustrates this interest: it lists more than 250 references to *Argyreia nervosa*.

FORMS AND PREPARATIONS

THE PLANT SOURCES OF LYSERGIC ACID AMIDES contain not just one psychoactive molecule. Several variations in effect are possible due to growing seasons and other environmental influences on the chemistry of the plant. In the American varieties of psychedelic *Ipomoea*, there is a uterotonic effect—hence these should not be used by pregnant women. It's a good idea to check as well to see if the seed company has added anything toxic to the seeds. This should be indicated on the package.

GRIND SEEDS

IN THE CASE OF THE *IPOMOEA* MORNING GLORIES, each seed is the equivalent of about 1 mcg. LSD; the usual dose lies between 100 and 200 seeds. Many early investigators failed to get any reactions at all. The reason in almost every instance was found to be that they had failed to grind the seeds first. The seeds should be ground to a flour before use. It's also a good idea to soak them in water—the psychoactive components are soluble—and then to strain the liquid through cheesecloth. The amides of value are in the liquid, which is ready for consumption.

DOSAGE

AS FOR THE BABY HAWAIIAN WOODROSE, the dose usually taken is four to eight seeds, although some users advise that no more than two or three should probably be taken the first time. With Hawaiian Woodroses or Morning Glories, high dosages are not advisable—beyond a certain

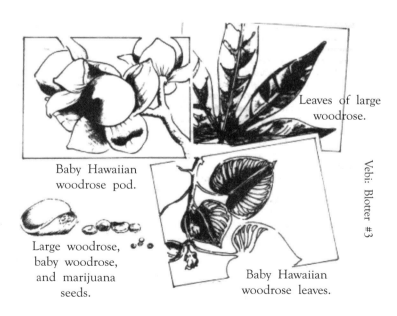

Leaves of large woodrose.

Baby Hawaiian woodrose pod.

Large woodrose, baby woodrose, and marijuana seeds.

Baby Hawaiian woodrose leaves.

Vebi: Blotter #3

level, experience so far has shown a tendency for limbs to get bluish. From reports I've seen, it's not clear whether the seeds had been dissolved and the amides strained out before ingestion.

Hofmann remarked that when he produced ALD-52, it had to be kept in solution and cold because it was quite unstable. Most of the other analogs have been tried by only a few people in research studies and have almost never appeared on the black market. A methylated form that produces LSD-type effects lasting only four to six hours has been distributed in Europe.

LSD appears in crystalline, liquid, and many other forms. As a crystal, a substantial dose can barely be seen by the naked eye. Usually, it is dissolved in ethyl alcohol or another solvent and then dropped onto a carrier, usually blotter paper.

DOSES VARY

WHEN SANDOZ DISTRIBUTED LSD, it delivered it in sealed vials or in bottles of calibrated dosage from which precise amounts could be removed by syringe. Such quantitative, not to mention qualitative, care hasn't appeared yet in the black market.

More than a few users have discovered considerable differences in the dosage of blotters on the same sheet of paper. Some acid

Crystals of ergotamine—
the precursor used to make LSD
after extraction from ergot fungus.

is strong enough to provide four trips from a single tab or blotter, while in other instances the amounts are in the range of 25 to 50 mcg. per blotter.

Ergot was the starting material used until the early 1960s. At the beginning of that decade, the Farmitalia Company of Milan, Italy developed a method for growing this fungus in vats of *Claviceps paspali.* It offered this for sale at $10,000 per kilogram until well past the mid-1960s, when such work was suspended.

In *The Psychedelic Reader,* Gary Fisher described dosage levels for psychotherapeutic sessions as being quite high, generally over 250 mcg. He also touches on the use of other drugs in conjunction with LSD, particularly small amounts of amphetamine and psilocybin as initial pretreatment.

DETERIORATION

LSD DETERIORATES SLOWLY OVER TIME, oxidizing into iso-LSD. In about a decade, potency decreases by about half. Some writers have exaggerated the deterioration involved. It does, however, disintegrate rapidly in the presence of light, oxygen, and moisture.

PURITY TESTS

M OST CHEMICAL TEST KITS ADVERTISED BY MAIL ORDER for checking out alleged psychedelics generally rely on the Keller and van Urk-Smith color-change tests. In these, the sample to be examined is poured into a reagent with the resulting color then compared with standards

Purity Tests & LSD

All derivatives of lysergic acid give characteristic color reactions based on the indole nature of lysergic acid .... A solution of traces of a lysergic acid derivative in glacial acetic acid, containing a small amount of $FeCl_3$, when added with concentrated H_2SO_4 develops a brilliant violet-blue color (Keller reaction). In the procedure of van Urk-Smith a solution of p-dimethylamino-benzaldehyde in diluted sulfuric acid containing traces of $FeCl_3$ is mixed with an equal volume of the lysergic acid derivative in tartaric acid solution. A violet-blue color appears. Whereas the Keller reaction is used mainly for qualitative identification, the van Urk-Smith reaction was standardized and can be used for quantitative determinations.

—Albert Hofmann

These test kits are useful in determining whether the substance in question is an indole or not. Melting point apparatus is also a rather crude indicator, although valuable as well in finding negative results.

THIN-LAYER CHROMATOGRAPHY

MORE SOPHISTICATED DETERMINATIONS CAN BE MADE with thin-layer chromatography, a process that is still quite inexpensive. In this technique, the substance to be tested is placed at the bottom of a coated plate and then creeps up through a solvent for ten to fifteen minutes. Various psychoactive components then locate themselves in specific positions and exhibit coloration depending upon the solvent used, and thus can be identified as specific compounds. LSD-25, in a typical reaction, travels about halfway up the gel, where it takes on a bright yellow appearance. The position of iso-lysergic acid diethylamide, by way of contrast, lies right below. Use of different solvents, while assaying the same substance, can be almost as specific as the results derived from high-end equipment.

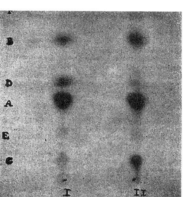

Chromatographs of alkaloidal extracts of Turbina corymbosa (I) and Ipormoea violaces (II).

Experience in making thin-layer discriminations is needed, however, since the eventual reading depends upon color distinctions and accurate measurements of resting locations. Gunk from a floor, bits of an eraser, various dyes and even milk have on occasion been thought to have tested out positively by some who have tried color-change tests. Difficulties in relying on verbal descriptions are evident.

Definition of Onionskin Pink

A light brown that is stronger and slightly redder and darker than alesan; stronger and slightly yellower and darker than blush; lighter, stronger and slightly redder than French beige; and redder, stronger, and slightly lighter than cork.

—Webster's Dictionary

OTHER TESTS

E.G.C. CLARK'S *ISOLATION AND IDENTIFICATION OF DRUGS* speci-
fies a method for making "microtests" of a "pedant drop"
or "microdrop." The sulfuric acid-formaldehyde testing of
DMT, to illustrate, yields dull orange with a sensitivity of
1.0 mcg. sensitivity, while the ammonium molybdate test
yields blue going to green and then yellow with a sensitivity of 0.1 mcg.

More precise testing is made by column, gas or high-
performance chromatography equipment, or by use of
magnetic resonance or an electron microscope. These
methods are all quite expensive and necessitate equipment
rarely available outside of industry, universities and crime
labs.

In gas chromatography, a sample is introduced into an
inert stream of gas flowing through a tube. Through
heating, it is broken down into its constituents which are
then carried by the gas depending upon how heavy they
are. Results are evaluated electronically in terms of nuclear
weights and compared with an appropriate standard.

High-performance liquid chromatography doesn't
involve a heating process, which can alter the original
substance. Accessibility to this machine and others even
more specific is rare, however. These matters are raised
here to indicate how difficult it is to establish the purity
of a psychedelic substance with certainty.

Hewlett-Packard
mass selective detector
used to analyze drug samples

TRENDS

PSYCHEDELICS WILL CONTINUE TO BE VIEWED as important agents of personal, psychological, cultural, and social change. Even in the face of enormous cultural tides in which they now are thought to cause barely a ripple, many individuals steadfastly devote their energies, resources, and even their lives to the investigation and propagation of the mysterious powers of these substances.

ORGANIC PSYCHEDELICS

THERE IS CONTROVERSY around an issue known as "the organic/synthetic debate." Ralph Metzner, Andrew Weil, Terence McKenna, and others argue that psychedelic plants can be used more beneficially because the wisdom derived from millennia of involvement with such species has resulted in shamanic traditions of safe and conscientious usage. These ancient traditions serve as valuable paradigms for the use of psychedelics in contemporary Western culture—that lacks established rituals for such practices.

Laboratory extracts and synthetic analogues have greater potency than natural sources and, therefore, may present greater risks. The history of usage of psychoactive

Ralph Metzner

plants, on the other hand, has convincingly established their physiological and psychic compatibility with the human organism—and possibly has even evolved into a harmonious relationship between human beings and the sentient fields of energy or "plant devas" that many believe permeate the traditional psychedelic botanicals.

By contrast, Alexander Shulgin, Dennis McKenna and Bruce Eisner argue that the distinction between the two is not particularly meaningful on a practical level. Many poisons are found in plants—some in significant concentrations in certain traditional organic psychedelics. The view is succinctly summarized in an issue of *Psychedelic Monographs and Essays*: "A molecule is the same whether it is created in a plant or animal or in laboratory glassware. LSD is semi-synthetic, and strychnine is natural. Does that mean that LSD is bad and strychnine is good?"

Mind States Conference

PICKING UP WHERE THE STANFORD BRIDGE CONFERENCE OF 1991 left off, the Mind States Conference was launched in 1997 and became an annual event in 2001—sometimes meeting in Berkeley, sometimes in Jamaica. The purpose was to explore the continuing perspective on altered consciousness.

The 2003 session held at the International House, near the University of California campus in Berkeley, celebrated the 60th anniversary of the discovery of the psychoactive effects of LSD.

Speakers—Pablo Amaringo, Susan Blackmore, Richard Glen Boire, Erowid staff, fantasy artist Alex Grey, Stanislav Grof, virtual reality genius Jaron Lanier, Ralph Metzner, David E. Nichols, artist Stevee Postman, Nicholas Sand, Zoe Seven, Ann and Sasha Shulgin, R.U. Sirius, Myron Stolaroff and other psychedelic dignitaries—extoled upon the past, present, and future of these world-changing molecules—as they see them. They spoke on ayahuasca shamanism, memetics, "the contents of consciousness," the folk art of "blotter acid," the neurology of aesthetics, future mind technology, virtual reality, cyber-punk literature and so forth.

HIGH TECH CONNECTION

MANY WHO ARE INTERESTED IN PSYCHEDELICS—thereotically and experientially—have considerable enthusiasm for high technology and human-computer interface. *Mondo*, a briefly-lived magazine, epitomizied the intersection between psychedelics and electronics. Its issues regularly featured articles discussing psychochemicals side-by-side with computer hacking, virtual reality, and brain-machines.

The alliance of high technology and psychedelics might seem odd to those who remember the psychedelic culture of the late 1960s, often characterized by an anti-technological "back to the land" philosophy and an attempt to return to tribally-rooted lifestyles. The retrospec-tive approach persists as an unmistakable thread in the increasingly varicolored tapestry of contemporary psychedelia, weaving images borne of widespread fascination with shamanic practices, organic psychedelics, and goddess-oriented post-feminist spiritual-ity.

There are probably twenty-five million Americans who have taken LSD, and who would, if hard pressed in private, also tell you that it profoundly changed their lives, and not necessarily for the worse. I will readily grant that some of these are hopeless crystal wor- shipers or psychedelic derelicts creeping around the Oregon woods. But far more of them are successful members of society, CEOs, politicians, Buddhist medita-tion teachers, ministers, and community leaders. This is true. Whether we want it to be or not.

—John Perry Barlow

However, this revivalist strand is interwoven with an enthusiastic embrace of the scintillating electron web of new digital culture. This trend was evident in the Mind States Conferences.

When asked to speculate on why developments in virtual-reality technology so consistently rivet the attention of psychedeli-cally-oriented people, it has been suggested that there is a resonance between the multiple realties experienced in psyche-delic states and the multiple realities available to the skilled pilot of virtual-reality equipment.

The realities revealed to psychedelically-enhanced perception are to a greater or lesser degree the creation of the user's consciousness. Virtual reality technology allows its pilots to bathe the sensorium in a pool of information designed according to their own specifications, thereby providing "a way to experience this alteration of reality in a much more organized fashion," as Bruce Eisner put it.

Culture—Counterculture

There have always been two strands in psychedelic culture and counterculture. A majority strand of people felt overwhelmed by the ugliness of Western civilization and wanted to get as much distance from it as possible. But about ten percent always consisted of "sci-fi" types. For instance, Digger manifestoes of '67 and '68 anticipated "machines of loving grace" that would usher in a post-scarcity culture.

—R.U. Sirius

Virtual reality is a manifestation of the increased blurring of the distinction between "solid reality" and the stuff of dreams, thoughts, and the mind. The malleable, rapidly transmuting world into which we're moving is one in which acidheads should have a distinct type of advantage, having already experienced the plasticity and variability of the realities of the mind.

The growing trend towards technology is an inevitable recognition on the part of intelligent people that something unprecidented is happening and there's something quite irresistible about it. Electronic technology is bringing about a realization of the kinds of visions you have on

Dan Joy

R.U. Sirius

psychedelics—of a global brain or nervous system. This link-up is happening naturally—and technology is one of the ways we're getting there.

Bruce Eisner

Eisner explains, "I view psychedelics and virtual reality as potentially highly synergistic. Virtual reality could become the ultimate programmer of the psychedelic experience. Set and setting could be created from scratch, using computer-human interface."

Non-Drug Drug

I feel that it is inevitable that in the future, the pharmacology we have learned from ingesting plants is going to blur with a better understanding of the pharmacology of experiences. As we develop virtual-reality devices of such high resolution that you can put on a piece of equipment and enter a reality as convincingly real as this one, one of the possibilities is to actually monitor neurotransmitter release at the synaptic level, and relate that to the sequences of experiences that are presented.

And through that process, it's possible to develop sequences of experiences that produce certain neurotransmitter release patterns across individuals. So you have an experience that produces a change in the brain the way that a drug might produce a change in the brain. You begin to develop a non-drug pharmacology.

—Richard Yensen

Leary traveled the lecture circuit in the 1990s talking of the high-tech future. He explained his interest in digital-imagery technology by citing "the power of visual signals to re-imprint the brain. The eyes are the windows of the brain. The rods and cones of the visual apparatus are made of nervous tissue; they are actually extensions of the brain itself. The brain starts with dilated pupils."

Leary with virtual reality
glove & visual mask.

Leary predicted the development of "personalized, hand-held digital-imagery devices that will empower the individual to control her own visual imprinting process. He empahsized that "The human brain is where the real power is. The value of electronic communication technologies is that they can link up human brains."

CHAOS THEORY

ASIDE FROM DIGITAL TECHNOLOGY, another cutting-edge scientific arena that has sparked tremendous fascination within psychedelic culture is that of Chaos Dynamics. This new theory is being fruitfully applied to a vast array of natural, social, historical, and even psychological phenomena. The argot of this scientific paradigm and its computer-generated fractal images—visual expressions of the mathematical equations that constitute chaos theory—are a regular feature at most gatherings of the psychedelically minded.

The visual resonance between fractal and psychedelic imagery is contributing to the psychedelic culture's embrace of the paradigm of chaos in very subtle ways.

UC Santa Cruz professor Ralph Abraham, Ph.D., a pioneer of chaos mathematics, publicly acknowledged LSD as a major tool and source of inspiration in his work. Perhaps it is no coincidence, then, that many experienced psychedelic voyagers attest to the fact that fractal graphics bear an uncanny resemblance to the visual imagery observed under high doses of LSD and other psychedelics. Abraham noted that fractals tend to confirm the intuition of many psychedelic users that they're not "hallucinating," but observing something significant and real.

Fractals

Fractal imagery may be providing psychedelic people with an affirmation of the validity and relevance of the psychedelic experience. Fractals have been found to be accurate representations of many phenomena and processes in nature.

Consciousness is a natural phenomenon as well. At least some of the processes occurring in consciousness may also someday be successfully modeled by fractal equations. This supports the idea that much of the psychedelic experience may be a matter of consciousness observing itself.

—Ralph Abraham

Many believe that LSD and other entheogens psychedelically fuelled the inspiration among Silicon Valley's high tech pioneers and the amazing, but brief dot.com phenomenon. Supporting this observation, booksellers identified a new and fertile group of book buyers— "Bohemian Boomers." These Baby Boomers are high tech oriented, interested in spiritual developments and mind-expansion.

BURNING MAN

BURNING MAN IS A KIND OF 21ST CENTURY ACID CELEBRATION. Throughout the 1990s and on into the 2000s each August, some 25,000 people coming from around the world made a journey to the Black Rock Desert to spend a week being part of an experimental community, which challenged its members to express themselves and to rely on themselves to a degree that is not normally encountered in day-to-day life.

Community, participation, self-expression and self-reliance are the tenets of the Burning Man experience which culminates with the burning of a ever-taller wooden man. While taking psychedelics is not promoted, its influence is readily evident in the philosophy, the art and the behavior of the tribe that gathers.

The first burning man event was put on by Larry Harvey with help from Jerry James, in 1986 on Baker Beach in San Francisco and was attended by 20 people. The man to be ritually burned was eight foot tall. From those early days, it evolved into a bustling city in the middle of a bleak ancient desert lake bed, known as the playa—a city in the desert, dedicated to radical self-reliance and radical self-expression.

We Need Rituals

Well, we don't have a lot of rituals in this society really. Well, we have some rituals in this society; we have football games, we have the Super Bowl.

But when the Super Bowl is over ,when a football game is over, you've had your thrill but suddenly you begin to realize that it was inherently meaningless. There was no transcendence....

—Larry Harvey
Ritual, Community and Burning Man

ACID ART

ART IS AN ESSENTIAL PART OF THE EXPERIENCE. Striking sculpture, installations, performance, theme camps, art cars and amazing costumes The art from Burning Man has been reviewed by many art magazines, including *Art Week, Public Art* and the *New Art Examiner*.

There are no rules about how people must behave or express themselves. It is up to each participant to decide how  they will contribute and what they will give to the community. "The giving of yourself is the greatest gift you can give to the Burning Man Community," according to the organizers. After the event ends and the area is cleaned, there is no trace of the city that was there just days before—revealing the ecological concerns traditionally shared by psychedelic enthusiasts.

Harvey determines a theme each year, to encourage a common bond to help tie each individual's contribution together in a meaningful way. Participants are challenged to find a way to make the theme come alive, whether it is through a large-scale art installation, a theme camp, gifts brought to be given to other

Larry Harvey

individuals, costumes, or another medium. There's always somebody there who's thought up something you've never even considered.

IMPACT

THE IMPACT OF THE BURNING MAN EXPERIENCE has been so profound that a culture has formed around it—a culture that pushes the limits of Burning Man and has led to people banding together nation-wide to put on their own events to rekindle that magical feeling that only the feeling of being part of this community can provide.

NEW PIONEERS

USE OF MIND-ALTERING SUBSTANCES IS AS OLD as civilization itself. Human—and animals, too—enjoy changing their minds in unusual ways. New psychedelic pioneers are emerging and we can expect more to follow them.

In an article about psychedelic use, the *Gentleman's Quarterly* wrote, "Part of the recipe for [creative] abundance is chemical. How should we react to it? ... as tolerantly and calmly as possible. As ever, the pioneers will continue to pioneer, assuming whatever risks they deem necessary. Judge them not by the trips they take but by the gifts they bring back."

PROFILES

Albert Hofmann holding a ling chi mushroom while doing Tai Chi.

ALBERT HOFMANN

IN THE DECADES FOLLOWING his invention of LSD, Sandoz Pharmaceuticals chemist Albert Hofmann continued to synthesize many compounds of significance in medicine. Several of these—notably hydergine used in the treatment of Alzheimer's disease and depression—have been derivatives of ergot, the same rye mold that provided the precursors for LSD. Hofmann has summarized his life and work in *LSD: My Problem Child* and authored *Plants of the Gods* with Richard Evans Schultes.

Well into his nineties, Hofmann continued to be a major global spokesman for the use of LSD as "a material aid to meditation aimed at the mystical experience of a deeper, more comprehensive reality." Many credit his influence with positively affecting Switzerland's recent decision to legalize the use of certain psychedelics in psychotherapy under specific conditions.

STANISLAV GROF

IN THE LATTER YEARS of the 20th Century, LSD researcher Stanislav Grof, M.D., and his wife Christina, developed a powerful and increasingly popular method of inducing psychedelic-like alternative states of consciousness known as "Holotropic Breathwork." This technique

Laughing Man

Stanislav Grof

does not involve the use of drugs, and is regarded by thousands of practitioners worldwide as an extraordinarily fast and effective psychotherapeutic modality.

The Grofs' research has given rise to a new map of the psyche and a re-classification of certain mental states, previously diagnosed as "psychotic," as "spiritual emergencies," or junctures of crisis in the pychospiritual healing process. In the early 1980s Christina Grof founded the Spiritual Emergence Network in order to provide various services to those undergoing such disruptive but potentially very integrative psychic episodes. The Grofs' new paradigm of mental health and its practical application are expressed in their book *The Stormy Search for the Self*.

BOB WALLACE

BOB WALLACE FOUNDED MIND BOOKS which rooted out and made available the best psychedelic books available. His ad-hoc bookstand would be found at the Mind States Psychedelic conferences and Burning Man. But Bob was more than a bookseller. He was a co-founder of Microsoft and retired with an undisclosed sum. He was devoted to helping psychedelic research and made regular large donations to organizations like MAPS. Still a young man in his early 50s, Bob got pneumonia and unexpectedly died in 2002, leaving the psychedelic community stunned.

Timothy Leary

TIMOTHY LEARY

ONCE THE PERSON MOST CLOSELY LINKED with psychedelics, in the public mind, right up unti his death in 1996, Timothy Leary continued to be a popular writer and lecturer who focused on the humanistically motivated development of educational technology.

In his last years he authored and participated in the development of eight pieces of educational computer software, including the commercially successful MindMirror, a tool for psychological self-analysis based on his ground-breaking 1950s textbook *The Interpersonal Diagnosis of Personality*. Leary maintained an arduous globe-spanning lecture circuit schedule, and was celebrated as a technological visionary.

Oscar Janiger

OSCAR JANIGER

JANIGER IS REMEMBERED for his eight-year naturalistic study on the clinical effects of LSD and his classic investigations in the 1950s and early 1960s on the role of LSD in the creative process. This latter program is noted for having involved many of that era's most celebrated talents as volunteer subjects.

Janiger channeled much of his time and energy into his role as co-founder of the Albert Hofmann Foundation, a nonprofit organization that opened an international library for the study of consciousness. Semi-retired from private practice, Janiger continued his work as a professor emeritus at UC Irvine Medical School. He authored *Private Practice: The Changing Role of Physicians in Contemporary Society*.

RALPH METZNER

RALPH METZNER worked with Timothy Leary and Richard Alpert on early psychedelic research at Harvard and edited the *Psychedelic Review*. He pursued research in altered states of consciousness and cross-cultural methods of consciousness expansion, and published

Ralph Metzner

articles on consciousness, shamanism, alchemy, transformation and mythology. Metzner is a professor at the California Institute of Integral Studies and maintains a private psychotherapy practice of psychotherapy. He co-founded the Green Earth Foundation, a non-profit educational organization devoted to healing and harmonizing the human relationship with the Earth.

Metzner's books include *The Psychedelic Experience, Maps of Consciousness, Know Your Type, Opening to Inner Light, The Well of Remembrance, The Unfolding Self, Green Psychology, Ayahuasca,* and *Teonanácatl: Sacred Mushroom of Visions.*

ROBERT MASTERS AND JEAN HOUSTON

IN THE MID-60S, THE HUSBAND-AND-WIFE RESEARCH TEAM of Robert Masters and Jean Houston had a vast impact on the understanding of psychedelics through the publication of a popular book titled *The Varieties of Psychedelic Experience,* which summarized the years of research in psychedelics and psychotherapy.

Influenced by the work of Alexander, Feldenkrais, and Erikson, Robert Masters has developed a technique of neural and sensory reeducation known as the Masters Psychophysical Method, of which there are hundreds of certified practitioners. Masters demonstrated that trances of up to seven or eight hours in duration can generate responses in the body and mind approximating those catalyzed by high doses of LSD. The heightened plasticity of the body and its receptivity to various therapeutic modalities under psychedelics makes the combination of bodywork and psychedelics a promising direction for possible future research.

Jean has become a major innovator of applied archetypal psychology in group contexts, a capacity in which she conducts seminars and consults with major corporations. She has served as a consultant in human and cultural development to the governments of 35 different nations.

They have authored over a dozen books, including *The Possible Human, The Search for the Beloved, Godseed,* and *The Hero and the Goddess: The Odyssey of Mystery and Initiation.*

RICHARD ALPERT

LEARY'S HARVARD RESEARCH PARTNER Richard Alpert became a major figure in the alternative spirituality movement in the United States and abroad. His "karma yoga" focused on providing spiritual service to the dying, particularly AIDS patients, and to the bereaved. He is a founding member of the Seva Foundation, which takes its name from the Sanskrit word for "service." This organization implements a wide variety of social-service programs worldwide. In collaboration with Paul Gorman, Alpert published a book on the subject of spiritually based service titled *How Can I Help?*

After adopting the Sanskrit title "Ram Dass"—or "Servant of God"—in the early 1970s, he became viewed as something akin to a spiritual guru by many Western seekers. Alpert modestly asserted that he is "a holy man only half the time." Humorously calling himself a "Hin-Jew," he sought to integrate his Jewish spiritual and cultural heritage with the Eastern forms of mysticism that he absorbed in his studies and travels after his early psychedelic experiences. Alpert always publicly acknowledged the role that psychedelics have played in his spiritual development. After his debilitating stroke in the early 2000's Alpert was confined to a wheelchair and had some difficulty speaking. Nonetheless, he continued to be a popular lecturer and always gave a memorable performance.

ROBERT ANTON WILSON

TIMOTHY LEARY CLAIMED that Robert Anton Wilson—his occasional literary and theoretical collaborator—has interpreted my rantings and ravings and droolings better than anyone else." Wilson's books *Cosmic Trigger* and *Prometheus Rising* are particularly noteworthy for their accessible treatments of Leary's eight-circuit model of the nervous system.

Dan Joy

Robert Anton Wilson

Wilson is well-known for a widely performed play titled *Wilhelm Reich In Hell* and his satirical fantasy novels, including *The Illuminatus Trilogy* (coauthored with Robert Shea) and *Schrodinger's Cat* Trilogy. His other books include *The Illuminati Papers, Quantum Psychology, Cosmic Trigger II,* and *Reality is What You Can Get Away With.* Robert Anton Wilson is loved for his ability to shape popular notions of psychedelics with his satirical and mind-blowing writing.

In the last decade, Wilson has continued to shape popular conceptions of the psychedelic experience with his prolific output of erudite, psychologically astute, satirical, and occasionally mind-blowing literary occult sleight-of-hand. After a few years of sojourn in Ireland, he returned to Santa Cruz where he continued a vigorous schedule of public speaking even after being confined to a wheelchair and walker.

JOHN CUNNINGHAM LILLY

John Lilly

JOHN LILLY BLAZED A METEORIC TRAIL in his early career in the 1940s and 1950s as a medical researcher, performing important studies of the human organism's ability to withstand conditions of extreme stress, such as high altitudes and acceleration.

Lilly's interest in the outer limits of human experience led him in the late 1950s to invent the isolation tank, a coffin-like box in which one floats in warm water in a condition of silence, total darkness, and zero gravity. The aim of this invention was to provide a near-ideal environment for studying the human mind itself, removed from all outside influences. As his first and most important subject, Lilly examined his own mind and consciousness in the tank while under the influence of rather large doses of LSD. His experiments with isolation loosely formed the basis for the popular book and movie *Altered States*.

Lilly was introduced to LSD in the early 1960s and performed important research into this psychedelic as part of a team including Dr. Sandy Unger and Stanislav Grof at Spring Grove Mental Hospital in Maryland. Eventually he took his experiments with this mind-changer to the isolation tank, leading to influential theoretical elaborations contained in *Programming and Metaprogramming in the Human Biocomputer*. He chronicled his life and research in *The Scientist*.

Dan Joy

Stephen Gaskin

STEPHEN GASKIN

"STEPHEN"—as Gaskin likes to be called—held a weekly session for hippies called "Monday Night Class" which met at the Family Dog Autorium in San Francisco. They gathered four times in the Summer of 1969 for picnics on Mt. Tam where hundreds of his followers dropped acid.

In 1970, Stephen and his followers launched off with about 100 psychedelically-painted buses to find "the land." Eventually they founded a successful alternative community based on hippy principles gleened from psychedelic tripping, called "The Farm" in Tennessee—a uniquely successful and long-lived communitarian endeavor founded on principles derived in part from psychedelic experiences. Unlike most of the other communes that dotted the American landscape in the late 1960s and early 1970s, The Farm, whose residents once numbered over a thousand, channelled much of their efforts toward various forms of social service in the United States and abroad.

Stephen, who continued his hippy tradition well into the 21st century, became an elder statesman of psychedelic culture. He was sought after as a lecturer and public speaker. His classic personal account of the psychedelic heyday of the late 1960s that later gave rise to The Farm were told in *Amazing Dope Tales*. Always a visionary, Gaskin founded the Rocinante Health Center, an alternative residential community for the elderly, which is located next to The Farm. He also authored *Cannabis Spirituality* and ran for president in 2000.

TERENCE MCKENNA

UNQUESTIONABLY FOREMOST among the new generation of public exponents of the potentialities of psychedelics is ethnobotanist Terence McKenna. With an academic background in art history and shamanism and several globe-spanning ethnobotanical expeditions now under his

Kathy Thurmon Carr

Terance McKenna

belt, McKenna was an extraordinarily eloquent and erudite writer, a bardic speaker. He focused particularly on the experiences generated by psilocybin mushrooms and ayahuasca within a shamanic context. "My testimonial," McKenna told his audiences, "is that magic is alive in hyperspace."

His loyal followers were shocked when he died at the height of his career of brain cancer. McKenna authored many books, including *The Archaic Revival*, and *Food of the Gods: The Search for the Original Tree of Knowledge*, a landmark examination of the role of plants in human history. His classic theoretical exploration, *The Invisible Landscape*, was written in collaboration with his brother, psychopharma-cologist-turned-ethnobotanist Dennis McKenna. McKenna and his wife Katherine founded Botanical Dimensions, an organization devoted to the preservation and propagation of endangered plant species of ethnobotanical interest.

Rick Doblin

RICK DOBLIN

RICK DOBLIN founded the Multidisciplinary Association for Psychedelic Studies, or MAPS, which promotes and sponsors scientific research into psychedelics. He authored a follow-up study to Leary, Alpert, and Metzner's "Good Friday Experiment," an early investigation into the relationship between psyche-delic and religious experience.

FAUSTIN BRAY

AT VIRTUALLY EVERY GATHERING of the psychedelic commu-nity photo-biographer Faustin Bray would be found tire-lessly recording all the goings on. Founder of Sound-Photosynthesis, Bray accumulated an amazing collection of lectures from the psychedelic gurus.

LAURA ARCHERA HUXLEY

WIFE OF ALDOUS HUXLEY, Laura Huxley became an important member of the psychedelic community in her own right. She was a frequent speaker at the annual Mind States conferences where, in her flamboyant hat, she would softly speak wise words. She is the author of the self-help book, *You Are Not The Target.*

Los Angeles Times

Laura Huxley

ALEXANDER SHULGIN

PSYCHOPHARMACOLOGIST Alexander Shulgin—Sasha—is the originator of over a hundred psychoactive compounds. Some claim that he trained many of the the underground chemists. He is the author of the highly controversial *PIHKAL: A Chemical Love Story* and *TIKAL*, which he published with his wife through Transform

Dan Joy

Sasha Shulgin

Press. These books are considered to be milestones of psycho-pharmacology and psychedelic literature and contain a novelized account of decades of pioneering research into the synthesis and effects of many mind-changing agents.

The Federal Government demonstrated their lack of appreciation for the Shulgins' work when they busted him in his home in the late 1990s and stripped him of his Federal licenses to possess, consume and study various controlled substances.

SEBASTIAN ORFALI

AS THE FOUNDER AND PUBLISHER OF AND/OR PRESS, Sebastian Orfali was a major force behind the birth of the independent publishing scene. And/Or Press, which crashed and burned after a hostile corporate take-over in the early 1980s, published the first edition of *Psychedelics Encyclopedia*. Along with his partner, Dr. Beverly Potter, author of several career books, he founded Ronin Publishing, which rapidly became the world's foremost publisher of psychedelic literature. After his death in 1997, Ronin continued Sebastian's tradition with a long list of psychedelic titles.

In 1994, Sebastian was the "mid-wife"—as he called his relationship to the books he birthed—to Leary's magnus-opus *Chaos & Cyber Culture*. Potter has gone on to acquire the rights to books by Timothy Leary and John Lilly, which are "translated" into a timeless upbeat internet style designed to appeal to new generations. Of the ever-growing list of new Leary titles, which include *Your Brain is God*, *Musing on Human Metamorpheoses*, *Change Your Brain*, *Politics of Self-Determination*, and *Politics of PsychoPharmocology*, Potter says, "Like L. Ron Hubbard, Tim Leary will continue to publish post-humorously!"

INDEX

BOOKS OF INTEREST

Badiner, Allan Hunt, *Zig Zag Zen: Buddhism and Psychedelics*, Chronicle Books, 02.

Beifuss, Will. *Psychedelic Sourcebook*, Rosetta, 96.

Black, David and Kenn thomas. *ACID: The Secret History of LSD*, Vision.

Brecher, Edward. *Licit and Illict Drugs: The Consumers Union Report on Narcotics, Stimulants, Depressants, Inhalants, Hallucinogens, and Marijuana - Including Coffee*, Little Brown, 72.

Cohen, Sidney and Richard Alpert. *LSD*.

Cohen, Sidney. *The Beyond Within: The LSD Story*, Encore Editions, 72.

Devereux, Paul. *The Long Trip: A Prehistory of Psychedelia*, Penguin, 97.

Dobkin de Rios, Marlene and Oscar Janiger, *LSD Spirituality and the Creative Process*, Park Street Press, 03

Emboden, William. *Narcotics Plants*, MacMillan, 80.

Grinspoon, Lester and James B. Backalar. *Psychedelic Drugs Reconsidered*, Bookworld Services, 97.

Grof, Stanislov. *LSD Psychotherapy*, MAPS: The Multidisciplinary Association for Psychedelic Studies, 01.

Hays, Charles.*Tripping: An Anthology of True-Life Psychedelic Adventures*, Penguin, 00.

Henke, James, Perry, Charles, Parke Puterbaugh, and Barry Miles. *I Want to Take You Higher: The Psychedelic Era 1965-1969*, Chronicle Books, 97.

Hoffer, Abram. *The Hallucinogens*, Academic Press, 67.

Hoffman, Albert & Richard E. Schultes. *Plants of the Gods*, Healing Arts, 02.

Hoffman, Albert. *LSD: My Problem Child: Reflections on Sacred Drugs, Mysticism, and Science*, JP Tarcher, 83.

Horowitz, Michael and Cynthia Palmer, (editors). *MOKSHA: Aldous Huxley's Classic Writings on Psychedelics & the Visionary Experience*, Inner Traditions, 99.

Hoskyns, Barney. *Beneath the Diamond Sky: Haight-Ashbury 1965-1970*, Simon & Schuster, 97.

Houston, Jean. *A Mythic Life : Learning to Live Our Greater Story*, HarperSF, 97.

Houston, Jean. *Mind Games the Guide to Inner Space*, Quest, 98.

Houston, Jean. *The Possible Human: A Course in Enhancing Your Physical, Mental, and Creative Abilities*, JP Tarcher, 97.

Huxley, Aldous. *Doors of Perception and Heaven and Hell*, HarperCollins, 90.

Huxley, Aldous. *Island*, Perennial Press, 02.

James, William. *The Varieties of Religious Experience: A Study in Human Nature*, Routledge, 02.

Kleps, Art. *The Boo Hoo Bible: The Neo-American Church Catechism and Handbook*, Neo-American Church of Taxas, 71.

Krassner, Paul. *Paul Krassner's Psychedelic Trips for the Soul*, High Times Books, 01.

Leary, Timothy, Ralph Metzner, and Richard Alpert, *The Psychedelic Experience, A Manual Based on the Tibetan Book of the Dead*, Citadel Press, 95.

Leary, Timothy. *High Priest*, Ronin, 95.

Leary, Timothy. *Psychedelic Prayers and Other Meditations*, Ronin, 96

Lee, Martin A. and Bruce Shlain. Acid Dreams: The Complete Social History of LSD: The CIA, the Sixties, and Beyond, Grove Press, 86.

Lyttle, Thomas (editor). *Psychedelics Reimagined*, Autonomedia, 99.

Masters, Robert and Jean Houston. *The Varieties of Psychedelic Experience: The Classic Guide to the Effects of LSD on the Human Psyche*, Park Street Press, 00.

McKenna, Terence and Dennis McKenna. *The Invisible Landscape: Mind, Hallucinogens, and the I Ching*, Harper san Francisco, 94.

McKenna, Terence. *The Archaic Revival: Speculations on Psychedelic Mushrooms, the Amazon, Virtual Reality, UFOs, Evolution*, Harper San Francisco, 92.

McKenna, Terence. *Food of the Gods: The Search for the Original Tree of Knowledge*, Bantam Doubleday Dell, 92.

McKenna, Terence. *True Hallucinations and the Archaic Revival*, Fine Com., 98.

Melecchi, Tony (editor). *Psychedelia Britannica*, Turnaround, 97.

Merkur, Dan. *The Mystery of Manna: The Psychedelic Sacrament of the Bible*, Inner Traditions, 00.

Metzner, Ralph (editor). *The Psychedelic Reader: Selections from the Psychedelic Review*, Citadel Press, 93.

Metzner, Ralph (editor). *The Ecstatic Adventure*, MacMillan, 68.

Metzner, Ralph. *The Unfolding Self: Varieties of Transformative Experience*. Origin, 98.

Perrine, Daniel. The Chemistry of Mind-Altering Drugs: History, Pharmacology, and Cultural Context, American Chemical Society, 96.

Perry, Paul and Michael Schwartz (editors). *On The Bus: The Complete Guide to the Legendary Trip of Ken Kesey and the Merry Pranksters and the Birth of the Counterculture*, Thunder's Mouth Press, 97.

Raven, Peter H., Ray F. Evert, and Susan E. Eichhorn. *Biology of Plants*, W H Freeman & Co., 99.

Ruck, Carl, Blaise Daniel Staples & Carl Heinrich. *The Apples of Apollo: Pagan & Christian Mysteries of the Eucharist*, Carolina Academic Press, 00.

Selvin, Joel. *Summer of Love: The Inside Story of LSD, Rock & roll, Free Love, and High times in the Wild West*, Cooper Square Press, 99,

Stevens, Jay. *Storming Heaven: LSD and the American Dream*, HaperCollins, 88.

Tart, Charles (editor). *Altered States of Consciousness*, Psychological Processes, 92.

Wasson, R. Gordon, Albert Hofmann, Jeremy Bigwood, Albert Hofmann, Jonathan Ott and Carl A.P. Ruck. *The Road to Eleusis: Unveiling the Secrets of the Mysteries*, William Dailey Antiquarian , 99.

Weil, Andrew. *Chocolate to Morphine: Understanding Mind-Active Drugs*, Houghton Mifflin, 83.

PETER STAFFORD

PETER STAFFORD has written extensively about psychedelics in the "underground press" and has appeared on many radio and TV events, along with public speaking, and was an editor of *Crawdaddy*—the first "rock" magazine. Peter is best known for his book, *Psychedelics Encyclopedia*, which appeared in three USA editions, as well as in German, Italian, Czechoslovakian and Russian. Peter lives in Santa Cruz, California, California. His website can be found by searching for "Psychedelics 101." His e-mail is blueneck60@hotmail.com.

Other books by Peter Stafford:

Psychedelic Encyclopedia

LSD —The Problem-Solving Psychedelic
Retitled in UK as *LSD in Action*
co-authored with Bonnie Golightly.

Psychedelic Baby Reaches Puberty